THE CATHOLIC PRIEST

MORE WILDSIDE CLASSICS

Dacobra, or The White Priests of Ahriman, by Harris Burland
The Nabob, by Alphonse Daudet
Out of the Wreck, by Captain A. E. Dingle
The Elm-Tree on the Mall, by Anatole France
The Lance of Kanana, by Harry W. French
Amazon Nights, by Arthur O. Friel
Caught in the Net, by Emile Gaboriau
The Gentle Grafter, by O. Henry
Raffles, by E. W. Hornung
Gates of Empire, by Robert E. Howard
Tom Brown's School Days, by Thomas Hughes
The Opium Ship, by H. Bedford Jones
The Miracles of Antichrist, by Selma Lagerlof
Arsène Lupin, by Maurice LeBlanc
A Phantom Lover, by Vernon Lee
The Iron Heel, by Jack London
The Witness for the Defence, by A.E.W. Mason
The Spider Strain and Other Tales, by Johnston McCulley
Tales of Thubway Tham, by Johnston McCulley
The Prince of Graustark, by George McCutcheon
Bull-Dog Drummond, by Cyril McNeile
The Moon Pool, by A. Merritt
The Red House Mystery, by A. A. Milne
Blix, by Frank Norris
Wings over Tomorrow, by Philip Francis Nowlan
The Devil's Paw, by E. Phillips Oppenheim
Satan's Daughter and Other Tales, by E. Hoffmann Price
The Insidious Dr. Fu Manchu, by Sax Rohmer
Mauprat, by George Sand
The Slayer and Other Tales, by H. de Vere Stacpoole
Penrod (Gordon Grant Illustrated Edition), by Booth Tarkington
The Gilded Age, by Mark Twain
The Blockade Runners, by Jules Verne
The Gadfly, by E.L. Voynich

Please see www.wildsidepress.com for a complete list!

THE CATHOLIC PRIEST

A GUIDE TO HOLY ORDERS

by
Bishop Karl Prüter

WILDSIDE PRESS

Copyright © 1993 by Karl Prüter

No part of this book my be reproduced in any form without the expressed written consent from of the publisher.

THE CATHOLIC PRIEST

This edition published in 2006 by Wildside Press, LLC.
www.wildsdepress.com

CONTENTS

PART I: PREPARATION

1. The Call to Holy Orders 7
2. The Priesthood of Jesus 13
3. The Role of the Priest in Public Worship 17
4. The Priest as Confessor and Counselor 23

PART II: TRAINING

5. The Priest as Preacher 35
6. The Role of the Priest at Weddings 39
7. The Priest as Missionary 45
8. The Priest as Healer 51
9. Preparation for the Holy and Priestly Life 57

PART III: PRACTICE

10. The Priest as Teacher 71
11. Father to the Parish 77

Note and Bibliography 82
Index 83
About the Author 88

PART ONE
PREPARATION

I.

THE CALL TO HOLY ORDERS

In a study on the nature of the priesthood, it would seem logical to begin with a definition of the priesthood. But that is not where most students of the subject begin. Those who study theology and the nature of Holy Orders are almost exclusively those who at one time or another experienced a call. To complicate matters a bit, it is hard to define the nature of Holy Orders when we have difficulty defining the call and understanding its implications. Talk to many ministers, priests, and rabbis, and you will be bewildered by the varied accounts of their experiences in receiving a call to serve God. Some came to their ministry by a call as vivid and as explicit as Paul's Damascus Road experience. Others felt a stirring within, and still others insist they had always known that they were called to serve God.

Further, if you have known these people for a long period of time, you will have discovered that their understanding of their call to the ministry frequently changed over the years. Almost all still believe they were called, but admit that their understanding of their ministry or apostolate has changed. To many this is disturbing and disconcerting, but if we go to the New Testament we will see parallels with the calls received by Paul and other ministers in the New Testament Church.

The fact is that God calls us not once but many times, and in many ways. Perhaps I can be more specific if I share my own experiences. When I was a sophomore in high school, I led a student strike and some 1,400 students were out for a week. At that time, I was a nominal member of the Lutheran Church. I went there because both my father and mother saw as their highest Christian duty the need to send their only son to Sunday school. I went, but I knew that when I grew up I would probably not go. My reason was simple. My Sunday school teachers taught me well. They taught me that Jesus said not only, "Thou shalt not kill," but he also said we must even love our enemies; the church members and the pastors that I knew did not accept it. The only reason, if it were expressed, was that they considered Jesus' teachings too impractical for this world, and since it is the only world we have that is a true dilemma. But someone did believe and care enough to present me with a life-changing challenge. A man named Jim Stringham, whom I had never met, came to call on me. He said he was a physician who had been with the Presbyterian Church in China and he wanted to tell me about his life and how Christ had turned his life around. I don't recall the details anymore, but he did say that when he had this encounter with Christ he felt led to return an umbrella that he had stolen. Then he invited me to go to a camp that the Oxford Group was holding in the Pocono Mountains in Pennsylvania.

The Oxford Group was founded by a Lutheran minister, Frank Buchman, and it taught that God would guide us if we would turn to him in prayer. As a standard of behavior it held that all the commandments would be upheld if we would be absolutely honest, unselfish, pure, and loving. While at the camp, I experienced what many would call a conversion. The Oxford Group prefers to use the term "changed." I saw that it did not matter that many thought Jesus's teachings were impractical. What mattered is that He asked me to live by those standards, and if Jesus asked me, surely it would be possible. Perhaps not possible on my own, but with the help of the Holy Spirit nothing is impossible. As a layman, I felt *called* to share these new-found convictions with others. Sometimes we forget that our first *call* to preach does and should come when we are called to be members of the church. For many this naturally comes at baptism or at confirmation, but the spirit moveth in strange and mysterious ways. It is noted in the New Testament that some disciples had not received the Holy Spirit although they had been baptized. So the disciples were moved to go to them and lay hands on them that they might receive the Holy Spirit. It does not say whether all those who received the laying on of hands did so, but if they all did, it was remarkable, since I feel that it doesn't always happen in modern confirmations. But that is not the point: calls come when God chooses, and when we are prepared to receive them. Also it needs to be emphasized that in the call to church membership we are called to preach the gospel.

We sometimes forget that, when the Holy Spirit spoke to the Church at Antioch, telling the church to set Paul and Barnabas apart and lay hands on them, Paul had already preached to many. The ordination was to set them apart. They were now members doing what members do, but they were also in Holy Orders, having received the Holy Spirit. Unlike the first call, the congregation is given knowledge of the call before the ministry begins. When Saul was first called, he alone knew of it. Later the Holy Spirit told Ananias, and still later the Church at Jerusalem. But in Antioch the order was reversed. In any case a call to the ministry is not private. When God tells an individual He also makes it known to the bishop and to the congregation. A true call does not take place in isolation but involves the whole church.

After I became identified with the Oxford Group, I tried to serve Christ and His church as an active layman. I felt guided by the Spirit to go to college and study journalism. Again, the call I felt was to become a journalist. This was, I thought, to be my vocation. Yet, in my third year of college, I felt drawn to the active ministry. I prayed about it and again I felt a call. This time I felt that I should become a minister in the Church in which I was raised. Does this mean my call to be a journalist was wrong? No, the training I received certainly became a part of my ministerial calling. The Holy Spirit merely brought me further revelation, perhaps as I was ready to receive and accept it.

One thing we must watch very carefully if we are to be led by the Holy Spirit. We must not run ahead of Him or read our own desires and wishes into what he tells us. As I went ahead and enrolled in seminary, I soon discovered two things. I had been led to a very fine school; the education I received there was the finest. I also soon learned that I was not a Lutheran and that if I sought ordination in the Lutheran Church I would encounter problems. Again, how did I go wrong when I thought I was guided by the Holy Spirit to serve the Lutheran Church as a minister? First, I had made some assumptions. Always dangerous! I assumed that because I had been reared as a Lutheran that this is where God wanted me. I never asked, although it is possible that this is where He did want me at that time. I had good training. So once again, I sought further guidance and again, I seemed directed into a place of temporary service. I became a minister in the Congregation Christian denomination. Here, I spent fifteen very fulfilling and happy years. I felt, I had found my place, and I worked hard and faithfully, but again because I was living in a changing world I was required to make yet two more major changes. The Congregational Churches united with the Evangelical and Reformed to create a denomination which I could not in good conscience serve. My first move was to serve with a small dissenting group. To do so, I had to become a parttime pastor. Also, I was moving from a church of three hundred members to a parish of about fifteen. I had to remind myself that "I was called to serve God by preaching the gospel and administering the sacraments." He never told me whether the number of people to whom I ministered had to be small or large. In the new remnant denomination, I found a few things lacking that seemed to me belonged to the complete Church. The lack of liturgical worship in most of the parishes seemed a rejection of Christ's command that we celebrate the Lord's Supper for His recalling. Again, I sought guidance and everything seemed to fall in place. I was directed toward the Old Catholic Movement and it seemed that God had prepared me in advance. During my years with the Congregationalists, I saw the need for liturgical worship, and during my time with the continuing remnant I had become a worker priest and realized that my ministry could be full even though I could not give a full day's service. I shared my new call with Archbishop Peter Zhurawetzky of Christ Catholic Church in the Americas and Europe, and he urged me to receive Catholic Orders and begin a Christ Catholic mission in Boston. My ordination took place in a small chapel in Rahway, New Jersey before a congregation of two—but I had no doubt that the Holy Spirit was present.

The Scriptural teaching regarding ordination and consecration is quite simple. Jesus consecrated the apostles (*Luke* 24:46-51) and we are told He lifted his hands and blessed them. He then commissioned them to preach his name among all nations, beginning at Jerusalem. Going back to the ordination of Paul: remember that before he was ordained at Antioch, he was first brought to the apostles that they might approve him. Christ Catholic ordination has three requirements. First, that a man receive a call, second that he be approved by a bishop in the apostolic succession who at the time of ordination will lay his hands upon him, and thirdly, that prior to his ordination he be known and approved by the members of the congregation among whom he has lived or who have examined him and feel called to invite him to serve as their pastor. The bishop should not ordain or place a man in a parish without prior consultation with the parish. God's revelation regarding ordination and consecration is not a secret, but is revealed to all concerned: the candidate, the congregation, and the bishop.

Ordination has no limits. A man is not ordained just for service in a particular congregation, but he is ordained for the whole church. Nor is he ordained for a specific length of time, but he is a priest forever. A laicized priest is nevertheless a priest, and his sacramental actions are valid even though he has been prohibited from exercising them. Although good order requires that all candidates for Holy Orders receive this three-fold call, occasions arise when a priest is found exercising the priestly office in a *de facto* manner.

In such cases, unless there are known impediments, the bishops should regularize the situation by ordination so that the priest will be a priest not only *de facto* but also *de jure*.

II.

THE PRIESTHOOD OF JESUS

Down through the ages many societies and many religions have had men called priests. Most of the leaders of pagan cults have been called priests and priestesses, and this, if for no other reason, makes many Christians uneasy about the term. As if this weren't enough, Jesus and the Jewish priests did not get along very well. The priests feared him as a rival and he, in turn, was critical of their oppression of the people.

Only in Paul's *Letter to the Hebrews* is Jesus referred to as a priest. To Paul Jesus is the high priest. If we read the gospels we discover that, although Jesus did not use the term, he did, indeed, regard himself as a priest. The fact that He did not use the term is not surprising, since Jesus refused to be labeled in many areas of his life. He avoided titles and he never explicity called himself the Christ, Messiah, Incarnate Word, Son of God, or Redeemer, yet he was all of these. Jesus recognized that if men can label you, by so doing they define who you are. For example, the word "Messiah" to many Jews meant a conquering king who would drive the Romans out of Israel. To other Jews, the Messiah as described in second *Isaiah* would be a suffering servant. Jesus, who more clearly fit the second image, was not about to let the proponents of the conquering king label him as Messiah, for to them the word had only one meaning and it did not describe Jesus.

When Jesus is described as a priest, the immediate picture that comes to most people's minds is that of the priests of the Temple at Jerusalem. Such a priesthood was not and could not be his. For one thing it was hereditary, and since he was not born into a priestly family, he could not be such a priest. Further, there was a difference of attitude. The priests of the Jewish faith saw themselves as rulers and were conscious of their privileged status. Jesus in preparing his disciples to take up their own priesthood sets before them the example of servant:

he who was to lead must first serve. Jesus is in no way hostile to the Jewish priests; in fact, he often sent people to the priests, so that they might fulfil their obligations to the temple. After he healed the leper, Jesus orders him to show himself to the priests so that they might certify the cure (*Matthew* 8:4, *Mark* 1:44, *Luke* 5:14, *Luke* 17:14). Nor does he regard the required offering as onerous but urges that it be given. Further on in his ministry he draws a picture which shows how he would set himself apart from the priests. The role of the priest in the story of the Good Samaritan is not a flattering one. Here he is telling his disciples that certain priests fail to understand their calling; the hero of his story is not a priest, nor a laywer, but a humble man, who was not of the Jewish faith but was a Samaritan.

As Jesus separated himself from the priesthood of his faith, he also separated himself from the Temple. I do not mean to imply that he did not worship there nor that it was his intention to abolish worship there, but he said he came to offer "something greater than the Temple" (*Matthew* 12:6). He offered *himself*, for God was in Jesus in a personal way that could not be duplicated by either the symbols, or the prayers, or the songs offered in the Temple. Jesus said regarding the temple, "Destroy this sanctuary, and in three days, I will raise it up" (*John* 2:19). The three days no doubt referred to his resurrection, but what sort of temple did he raise? The new temple, a spiritual one, would replace the material temple which had been the focal point of Jesus's religion. And in the new temple, he would be central. Not a building, but a person, the Son of God. People would come not only to worship God, but to be with God. Christ promised that whenever the Holy Supper was celebrated He would be present. I shall discuss this further when I talk about the Sacrament of the Mass.

Regarding Jesus's words concerning the Temple, it must be noted that at his trial before Pilate these words of his are twisted and misquoted. The priests of the Temple charge that Jesus has said that he will destroy the Temple. The reason for the indictment is obvious, for the priests saw that Jesus was challenging their authority and would substitute a new priesthood for their own. Pilate, too, saw in their charges a jealousy and a rivalry, and he did not intend to get caught in the middle (*Mark* 15:10).

No wonder Jesus avoided the term priest, since he did not wish to be seen as continuing the Temple priesthood. His was a new priesthood, and yet it did have its roots in the Hebrew tradition. In Matthew

22, in a discussion with the Pharisees, He asked them "What think ye of Christ?" (*Matthew* 22:42-45). In reply they say that he is the son of David, but Jesus says he is more. He says that David called him "Lord" and refers to the 110th Psalm. For what purpose? In the psalm David states that the Lord said of Christ, "Thou art a priest for ever after the order of Melchisedek." Why Melchisedek? Again Jesus sharply draws a distinction between his priesthood and the Temple priesthood. The latter is strictly a Jewish institution, while Melchisedek was a Gentile to whom Abraham paid tithes. Jesus is laying claim to a priesthood which is apart and of greater extent than the Temple priesthood.

A second distinction needs to be noted regarding the priesthood of the Catholic Church. It comes from Christ and is confirmed by the Holy Spirit. When Jesus was baptized, we are told that the Spirit of God appeared as a dove and said, "This is my beloved Son, in whom I am well pleased" (*Matthew* 3:17). This was Jesus's call, and to prepare himself for it, he went into the wilderness to spend forty days and nights. Unfortunately, we have a lot of preachers who also think they can get by with only forty days' preparation. They forget they are not Jesus!

If we accept the chronology of Matthew, when Jesus came out of the wilderness he heard the news of John's arrest. He then, seeing the urgency of his ministry, began to call his disciples. He first called Simon and Andrew and then the two sons of Zebedee, James and John. Note, He *called* them. So often ministers say they were called by the Holy Spirit, but it is always Christ who calls as he has promised, and it is the Holy Spirit who brings to the ordained the gifts needed for his ministry.

Judas was replaced by the apostles after they had prayed to the Lord, and had been given the names of two candidates, Joseph Barsabas and Matthias. Upon drawing lots they accept Matthias as the newly ordained apostle. The next recorded ordination comes after the events of Pentecost. The first deacons are ordained as recorded in *Acts* 6. It is followed by the best known "call" to the ministry: the calling of Saul (*Acts* 9). The call was definitely by Jesus Christ. This is the beginning of Saul's ministry, but there are many steps before his eventual ordination. First, Ananias is sent to him. He took Saul to Damascus and there had an opportunity to hear Saul's witness to the Jews in that city. Afterward he went to Jerusalem and there sought to join himself with the believers there. They, of course, feared him, but Barnabas took him and brought him to the disciples and vouched for him. Paul from henceforth was used by God and worked hard for the building of the Church. It was some time later that it was revealed to the church at Antioch that Saul and Barnabas were called to a specific ministry—this time by the Holy Spirit. For Jesus told his disciples that the Spirit would lead them. When it is clear what Paul and Barnabas are supposed to do, they are ordained and sent to Cyprus. They laid hands upon them that they might receive the gifts of the Spirit. But the ordination was a public ceremony, noting that Christ had called the men to the ministry, and invoking the Holy Spirit for the success of the ministry. What then is conveyed besides? Only that the men shall continue the priesthood which Christ himself had established, after the order of Melchizedek.

We believe that the Scriptures are clear: that Christ intended to establish a new priesthood, and a new temple. He is our high priest, and the Temple is His Body, that is, the Church. The Sadducees and the temple priests saw this and hence decided He had to be crucified. When they saw that it did not get rid of Him, they continued their opposition to the Church which He had established. At first the Christians continued to worship in the Temple and in the synagogues, but their first commitment was to Jesus Christ. They met in the synagogues wherever possible or in private homes on the first day of the week to celebrate Christ's resurrection and to meet with Him at the Holy Supper. Soon, they were driven out of the Temple and out of the synagogues, and the new Temple, the Body of Christ, became their only Temple, and Christ and His apostles, after the order of Melchizedek, their only priests.

A priest is primarily called to serve. He is the servant, not the master, of the congregation or parish. If a priest or a bishop is busy with administrative duties and cannot find time to care for his flock, he is not of the order of Melchizedek. This is the great distinction which Christ made and for which He is the great example.

III.

THE ROLE OF THE PRIEST IN PUBLIC WORSHIP

In each of the three major religions of the Western World a different answer would be given to the question, "What is the clergyman's principle role." A Jew would say that his rabbi must first of all be a scholar, an interpreter of the law. A Protestant thinks of his pastor as a preacher. He must be able to preach the World of God effectively. The Catholic or Orthodox layman looks to his priest as a faithful dispenser of the Sacraments.

The Catholic attends church to be with Christ at the Holy Mass, and if he is sick, or shut in, he expects his pastor to bring him the Holy Sacrament. In a Catholic Church the altar is in the center of the chancel and the pulpit at one side, to the left as we face the altar. That side has been designated as the gospel side. The opposite side is the epistle side. In many Protestant Churches the pulpit is in the center and you may even have trouble finding the communion table, although it is frequently in front and below the pulpit. The Protestant goes to "hear the Word" and the Catholic goes to be in the presence of Christ who is the Word.

The reasons why the Catholic Church has placed so much emphasis upon worship and the sacraments are many. First, it is Christ's command which he gave at the Last Supper that we should do this, in his memory, or as often translated, for "His recalling." To understand why he commanded it and why it is so important, we must examine carefully what took place on the night of the Last Supper.

It helps if we remind ourselves that Jesus and his disciples were Jewish and lived in a Jewish society. Many in the modern church seem to have forgotten this. For example, few of the people in the area where I live (the Ozarks) have ever been to a service in a synagogue. If they did, they would not think of it as the kind of service which Jesus and his disciples attended faithfully, but would actually feel it was "pagan." Can you imagine how they would feel if they attended a service like the many which were held in the Temple at Jerusalem? I know many fundamentalist groups in this area who are looking forward to the rebuilding of the Temple at Jerusalem. If and when it is rebuilt the liturgy and the incense will seem strange and almost alien to them. When they ask people to accept Jesus as Lord and Saviour they picture a gentile Jesus and not the Jesus who was at home in his Father's House that reeked of incense and where worship was the principle activity. At least they have heard of the synagogue and the Temple, but there are other important facts of Jewish life about which they know nothing. To understand the meaning of the Last Supper, we must know about another custom common among the Jews of Jesus's day; that is, the observance of the chaburah.

Like so many customs in the Middle East, it was connected with eating and drinking. It was based on the word "*chaber*" or friend. A chaburah then was a friendship meal and it simply involved a group of friends who came together regularly for a meal and to discuss some special devotion or charity. It might be a small group which met because of their common concern for the widows or orphans of the community, or for the maintenance of the local synagogue or even a cemetery. There were many of these chaburah and they developed similar rituals and rules. All meals in Jewish society had special prayers for various parts of the meal, and the chaburah had more than most. There was even a special prayer for relishes! Further, one's attendance at the chaburah made one a member in good standing, and to absent oneself for a long period of time was to disassociate oneself from the chaburah and the cause for which it was formed. Jesus and his disciples made up just such a chaburah, and on the night of the Last Supper they were meeting as they always had. Although it was Passover, the prayers were the prayers they had alwways said at their meals. However, one new element was added.

Jesus took bread and wine, the two most common foods in the Middle East, and made two astonishing declarations. First, as he took the bread he said, "This is my body which is broken for you" and in taking the wine he said, "This is my blood of the New Testament which is shed for many." The second declaration is a promise. He said, "This do for the recalling of me." It is one of the most important acts of his life. He is telling the disciples that the chaburah which they celebrated daily would continue. To come into His Presence they needed only to meet together as they always had, and share the friendship meal. He made it ever so simple by centering his words on just two common elements of the meal. Christians have experienced his presence at countless Last Suppers or Holy Communions in many churches and in many lands. Christians of many denominations are in agreement that Jesus Christ is ubiquitous. God is surely everywhere and everywhere to be found. But only at the Mass is he bodily present.

Now here come the theological problems. What do we mean by "bodily present" and what did Christ mean when he said, as he broke the bread, "This is my Body?" Was he referring to the bread or to the chaborah gathered before him? For would it not seem that it was broken when Judas betrayed Christ and He died upon the cross? Jesus wanted to assure them as they shared the bread that they would be forever together with Him. When he drank the wine, he similarly was not being literal, for the Jews were forbidden to drink blood. They could, however, drink wine and when they did they shared in his sacrifice on Calvary. If the wine is the symbol of his death, the bread is the symbol of his life.

It has been asked whether Jesus ever founded a church. The chaburah, was, is, and always shall be the Church. The Church did not give us the Lord's Supper. In a sense, the Lord's Supper and those who celebrate it have become the Church. You are a member when you are baptized or confirmed and invited to come to the Lord's Table. You are excommunicated when you either do not come to the Lord's Table or you are not permitted to come to the Lord's Table. That is why Paul was so concerned that we not come and eat and drink unworthily, for by partaking of the Lord's Supper we become members of the unbroken Body of Christ. For the Church is Christ's Body and Christ's Body is the Church. Beyond this we do not seek to explain the Lord's Supper more specifically. The doctrine of transubstantiation states that at the precise moment of the consecration the bread and wine become the Body and Blood of Jesus Christ. How do we know this? What we do know is that Christ is present at the Mass. We know this first because he has promised he would be, and secondly because countless Christians have experienced His Presence. This is what Old Catholics mean when they say they accept the doctrine of transubstantiation but not in the medieval sense. It is a paradox that the medieval mind wanted a rational explanation and was unwilling to accept the

Mass as a mystery. Today we are content to know that Christ is present at the Mass. We are content to let the how and in what form remain forever a mystery. We do not even know when Christ makes his presence at mass felt. We ring the sanctus bell at the epiclesis but this is arbitrary. Perhaps the faithful become aware of His Presence at different times during the mass depending on their readiness to receive Him.

In the early Church the Jewish rituals were performed by the Temple priests at the Temple and by the President of the synagogue at the synagogue. In some few cases the synagogue and its president accepted Christ and in those instances the regular rituals were performed by the president and he also became the president at the celebration of the Lord's Supper. In a few areas, such an arrangement continued through the first two centuries. However, in most areas the Christians were driven out of the synagogues, and their own ordained leaders conducted the old rituals of the synagogue, the prayers of the chabura, and the Lord's Supper. The Mass owes something to each, and it is the principle function of the priest to call the people to meet with Jesus at the Holy Supper. Together they sing hymns of praise and offer their prayers. Together they face the altar, where man and God have traditionally met. Together they seek direction merely by coming in the presence of Jesus Christ. "This do," he said, "in remembrance of me." And we should seek to do it as often as we are able.

At the Mass, or Lord's Supper, the priest reads the gospel narrative of the Lord's Supper. He breaks the bread, and in effect represents Christ. One reason for the eastern orientation is that it makes it easier to remove any question of the Mass being something between priest and people. It is always something that takes place between Christ and His people. The priest is also called upon to represent God in other sacramental situations. He is God's witness at marriage and at the Sacrament of Penance (confession). A priest does not marry people. No one is married by a priest, but before a priest. Neither does one confess his sins to a priest, but before a priest. The priest does not forgive sin, but pronounces to the penitent God's forgiveness and absolution wherever God's conditions for forgiveness are met, including true true contrition, restitution, and penance. The priest is not only an ambassador for God, but also for the parish, God's people. It is he who is most likely to be able to visit the prisoner, and the sick. He comes to the hospital bed to anoint the sick with oil, or to bring the Sacrament, and he represents both Christ and the congregation. It is in Christ's

The Catholic Priest

Name and the church's that he comes bringing gifts. Wherever possible the host he brings to the bedside should have been consecrated at the most recent mass held in the parish church, thus bringing the entire congregation together at this sacred meal.

While all members are instructed by Christ to go forth and preach and to baptize, it is most often the parish priest who fulfills these functions. Again, there is the matter of time. Baptisms should not be performed unless they are proceeded by instruction. Baptism calls for a commitment, either on the part of the baptized person, or, in the case of infants, on the part of parents and godparents. Perhaps we should add that the congregation too needs some instruction, for we solicit their support and few know what that means or how to give it. Again, I emphasize that a priest is called to be both pastor and teacher. We have too few pastors who fulfill both functions well.

I also realize that it may seem that I have strayed from my topic, the priest as leader in public worship. Yet, each of the other sacraments are connected with public worship. Even confession precedes every Mass proper and is a part of the Mass liturgy. When the priest offers Holy Communion to a hospital patient or a prisoner these visits are extensions of the Mass. The Sacrament is brought to all, that all may be united together in Christ. Today, Holy Anointing has been revived in the Church and has become a part of either the Mass or one of the other eight canonical hours. And it is charged to the priest to see that these things are done in an orderly and reverend fashion. In any event, I shall discuss each of the other sacraments and the priest's duties separately, but it is important to keep in mind that they are not separate from, but part of the worship we offer to God.

IV.
THE PRIEST AS CONFESSOR AND COUNSELOR

> *James 5:14. Is any sick among you? Let him call for the elders of the church; and let them pray over him, anointing him with oil in the name of the Lord: And the prayer of faith shall save the sick, and the Lord shall raise him up, and if he have committed sins, they shall be forgiven him. Confess your faults one to another, that you may be healed. The effectual fervent prayer of a righteous man availeth such.*

> *John 20:22-23. He breathed on them, and saith unto them, Receive ye the Holy Ghost. Whosoever sins ye remit, they are remitted unto them: and whosoever sins ye retain, they are retained.*

James has tied together the concerns of illness and sin. He does not say that illness is a result of sin, but he asks us to treat the whole man. When we as priests are called to a bedside to pray for the sick or to anoint the sick, we have not finished our ministry until we have heard the man's confession and offered absolution. Only then can the healing of body, mind, and soul be completed.

Fundamentalists have no great problem with the idea of "confess your faults, one to another," and often at public meetings share some very serious and intimate facts concerning many aspects of their lives. But in John we note that the forgiveness of sins was a specific charge given to his closest disciples. What is meant by the remission of sins? And how does the priest determine when he should pronounce that one's sins have been remitted and when must he withhold such a pronouncement?

First let us look at the role of the confessor. Catholics confess their sins to God and expect to receive forgiveness from God. Most frequently they confess their sins in private and silent prayer. They also participate in the General confession at the beginning of the Mass which is oral, but not specific. We pray for forgiveness for sins of commission and omission. God knows every detail of our life and does not need an enumeration. Finally, Catholics often go privately to the priest and before him confess their sins to God. They may choose to do this rather than rely on private or public confession for many reasons. One would be that they want to hear the assurance from the priest that they have met God's conditions in order to receive forgiveness. For forgiveness is conditional. We must be truly sorry for our sins, we must resolve not to repeat them, and we must make restitution wherever possible. If, for example, you steal a book from the library, you must not only feel contrite and resolve not to do it again, you must also return or pay for the book.

Of course, not all of our sins are so easily dealt with. If you slander your neighbor, how do you make restitution? You may ask him to forgive you, and you may even set the record right with many of those to whom you gave the false witness. But by then the story may have been told and retold so that it is no longer possible to set the record straight with scores of people whom you may not even know. A good confessor will help sort out the problem and help the sinner see when he has done all he can, and then by offering absolution and pardon assure the penitent of God's forgiveness. In addition to receiving assurance of God's forgiveness many penitents go also to the priest that he might instruct them regarding the proper penance for sins. For surely if we are sorry for our sins, in addition to making restitution we shall want to do something to atone for our sins. We know that Christ has already atoned for us, but we choose to be partners with him in that atonement for our sins. It is not always possible to make restitution. A drunk who injures someone seriously can seldom make restitution. If he has crippled a child, restitution is truly impossible. But he *can* perform penance by perhaps working in an institution for the care of crippled children or by contributing to its support.

Unfortunately, the Roman Church has for centuries had a system of penance that did little for the penitent and benefited no one else

The Catholic Priest

in particular. It was almost routine prior to Vatican II to have priests tell penitents to say five Hail Marys, two Lord's Prayers, or some similar penance. How can saying any prayer be thought of as a penance, which by definition is a punishment or a penalty? Prayer is always both a joy and a privilege. One might prescribe prayer as a reward but never as a punishment.

It is the priest's task to hear the penitant's confession, and to make certain he is sorry for his sin, intends to mend his ways, has made restitution where possible, and will undertake an appropriate penance for his sins. Then and then only will he be able to give assurance that God has indeed forgiven him his sins and will through the Holy Spirit strengthen and sustain him in his resolve to live a more Godly life.

While rooted in the New Testament, the Sacrament of Confession has undergone many changes down through the centuries. We trust that the Sacrament has only been altered as a result of the leading of the Holy Spirit. The Church has sought direction from time to time as problems have arisen in connection with this sacrament. For example, in the early church the public confession was often very explicit and because of this a great deal of disharmony arose in many congregations. While the changes that were made seemed logical, it was only after much debate and prayer that two important modifications were made. The first was the introduction of the general confession allowing the penitents to offer in silence before God alone any explicit details. Secondly, wider use of private oral confession before the priest provided the penitent an opportunity to receive a personal absolution and to avail himself of the counsel of the priest.

There are still some changes to be made in various branches of the Catholic Church. In the Roman Church the confessional booth is still retained, but many parishes are offering the penitent the opportunity to confess before a priest face to face. In Christ Catholic Church, we have adopted a practice which is unique to our branch of the Catholic Church. The priest is asked at the close of every confession to ask two questions. The first, "Do you feel that your state of spiritual health is better than it was a year ago." If the answer is "No" the penitent is well aware that he needs to make changes in his life and can seek the priest's help in adopting new disciplines and in monitoring his spiritual life more closely.

The second question is in a similar vein. It is "Do you have any problems that continually defeat you for which you would like to have me offer prayer or counsel?" Here the priest offers both intercessory prayer and his good office as a pastoral counselor. It certainly answers the critics who state that Catholics only have to confess their sins and go on sinning. Some may, but the Church strives to keep it at a minimum. And certainly those who never have to confess to God before a priest have even less incentive to amend their ways. Finally, the priest must take a pastoral view of confession and get across to the penitent that when God's conditions are met, His pardon and absolution are unconditional. It is equally important that the priest offer this assurance only when in good conscience he can do so. For the Penitent needs to known two important certainties: first, that when the priest gives the assurance of forgiveness God has actually forgiven him; and, secondly, that when he confesses before a priest his confession will be known to no one but God and the priest. The confidentiality of the confessional booth has been preserved down through the ages, and people of many faiths have been known to seek out priests, certain that neither court nor bishop nor any other person can force a priest to divulge their confession.

It is said that confession is good for the soul, and so it is. But it is also good for the mind, and psychiatrists, not always friendly to the church, will readily grant the healthful effects of regular confession. Further, they are aware that in dealing with guilt the priest can offer a person more than they can do for themselves. It is the priest to whom people turn for God's assurance of pardon. While not all the parishoners' problems can be dealt with in the confessional booth their solution may have its beginning there. The priest is frequently called upon for more counsel than can be afforded in the short time spent in the confessional.

Christ Catholic Church has a particular concern about the role of the priest as counselor. During the past fifty years the number of priests and ministers in the United States has dropped by about 75,000. But in the same period the number of psychiatrists, psychiatric social workers, and psychologists has increased from 14,000 to 150,000. It is evident that the pastor's job is now being assumed by new schools of therapists. The reasons for it go back to the early 1950s. At that time the church was shaken by a new revival of interest in pastoral care. At the time, I expressed concern about the direction in which the revival was headed. The traditional concerns were there, but the methods which were introduced were questionable. There was a new concept of the ministry, and under the cloak of a new nomenclature the function changed. Instead of the traditional designation "the cure of souls" clerics began to talk of pastoral psychology. In no way can the two terms be equated. The direction has not changed from the '50s, although a few of us have raised our voices in dissent. I firmly believe that the present practices are not theologically sound, and that they have been responsible for the decline in the number of people who turn to their pastors for counsel. When I first began in the ministry about half of the people who came to me for counseling were not active members of any church. Further, they had not been to any other counselor. In short, I was the counselor of first choice. In more recent years, people who have come into my office for help have already seen one or more secular counselors. They come, in part, because they have not found the help they sought, sometimes because they have run out of money to pay for secular counseling! They may not think pastoral counselors are all that good, but at least they're cheap. How did we ever get ourselves in this position?

The problem was created by pastors who eagerly and naively embraced many of the new techniques. A lot of pastors wanted to be psychologists, and wound up becoming amateur psychologists rather than professional pastoral counselors. In ignoring the great traditions of the past, pastors discarded proven ways of helping trouble souls. In exchange they bought into a lot of new theories and methods which often do not work. Pastors above all people should not have sold their birthright for a mess of pottage. A further tragedy is that many of the proponents of current counseling methods are unaware of the wealth which they discarded when thy turned their backs on the traditional care of souls. Dean Blakemore, one of the pioneers of the new counseling methods, has stated that, "Unfortunately, historical theologies are not of great help, since they pay attention only to two aspects of the relationship, namely preaching and worship." Here lies the crux of our problem. We have in this generation of priests and ministers a reasonable knowledge of what our forebears had to say about preaching and worship, but we do not know what they had to say about the more personal relationships between pastor and people. There is a mine of material from the past in both the Catholic and Protestant traditions that can be of help in meeting and dealing with every possible parochial problem.

Unsurpassed to my mind is a book written for both the counselor and for the client by Jeremy Taylor. Only the title is obsolete. *Holy Living and Holy Dying* is a book of devotions which contains an abundance of material that is actually preparation for counseling. Jeremy Taylor did not think that he had answered all the problems of conscience, but he did attempt to answer many and thus relieve the over-busy pastors of the task of dealing with the more obvious cases. What Taylor accomplished was to provide millions with a book that prepared them for the kind of counseling they would receive from the pastors of his day, if they had need for further consultation.

Although not a Catholic, Taylor's theology had deep Catholic roots and his book and methods were acceptable to the church both within and without the establishment for over a century. I believe that men like Jeremy Taylor, William Baxter, Martin Luther, and Jokob Gotthold perfected an ancient art and used it more effectively than anyone since apostolic times. The casuistry of the past was, at the least, readily learned by both pastor and people. In the latter part of the sixteenth century and the early part of the seventeenth century, more people than at any time in history went to their pastors as counselors and guides. They went first because nearly all pastors were steeped in like traditions and were able to give spiritual comfort that was expected of them. They not only had strong theological convictions but they also practiced, basically, the same theology. The people went secondly because they understood better than at any time the functions of the pastoral office and knew what to expect from an interview with their pastor.

Now that alone is an achievement of major importance, and we cannot ignore a technique so easily learned and so widely understood. It is a recognized problem of the new "pastoral psychology" that it must be "sold" to the people of the parish, and the selling job in many parishes has gone very poorly indeed. In the September 1950 issue of *Pastoral Psychology*, no less an authority than Russell L. Dicks wrote in an article entitled, "Telling the Story of Pastoral Care to the Parish," that the movement had a hard selling campaign in order to gain acceptance. Dr. Dicks noted "consumer resistance" and the fact that much of the minister's work in the field is confidential, and therefore not available for a selling campaign. Dicks was just plain wrong. People instinctively see that psychotherapy is alien to the church. He also missed

The Catholic Priest

the point that the traditional approach to counseling was more easily learned in any parish than the newer psychological approach.

The pastoral ministry of the post-Reformation period was so successful because it was firmly rooted in theology. The men often did what Dean Blakemore regarded as an oversimplification, that is, move directly from theological statements to the problem which brought the client into the pastor's study or the confessional. I do not say that phase of their technique can be carried over in our day, because people today frequently have too little respect for the doctrines of the church. In fact, they know little about the doctrines of the church. Nevertheless, all pastoral counseling must be done against a theological backdrop, against which every problem is seen and studied and from which a solution is drawn.

It seems to me that the newer methods of counseling do not give sufficient emphasis to the priest's theological resources. Seward Hiltner has apparently given considerable thought to the place of the minister's convictions and with much of what he says I can agree. However, I was surprised to read in one of his articles that we have a choice between what he calls the "legalistic" position and what Hiltner would regard as deeper and more "person-centered" views. Perhaps this is the key word. The counseling situation should not be "person-centered" but God-centered. Although the priest is called to minister to people, he may never forget that he ministers to people in the Name of God. God is always at the center of whatever he does. In the pastor's study there needs to be a crucifix that will remind both pastor and client that neither of them is central, but that God is central and it is He who is the source of help.

Many years ago, a Protestant pastor of my acquaintance was confronted with a wave of narrow and vicious gossip in his parish. His approach to the problem might be looked upon by today's counselors with horror, but Jeremy Taylor would have understood it. To those outside of the church, his approach was primarily one of showing friendly interest and counseling with their basic problems only when his assistance was sought. Now in the case of idle gossip, it is seldom that any amount of preaching will bring those involved to an acknowlegment of their sin, or to the pastor's study. The pastor forgot for a moment all he had learned about non-directive counseling, and sent notices to the people involved, asking that they see him individually in his study before the next celebration of the Lord's Supper. When each individual arrived, the pastor asked them kindly but firmly whether he intended to receive communion and if so instructed him to make certain that he was properly prepared before so doing. In every case, the problem of bearing false witness was faced, and all upon being instructed that they could not break the commandment against false witness and be in communion with the church made their confession, repented, and gave their promise that they would not repeat the offense. When the choice was put before them, each made his choice and chose to remain in communion with the church.

Call it legalistic, call it authoritarian; I firmly believe it is neither, but clearly the pastor's duty to see that his people understand what is involved when they participate in the sacraments. As religious counselor, he alone can advise in this area, and to be true to his calling, he must; yet isn't this one of the areas that has been so long neglected in the church?

The post-Reformation counseling was successful because of the Protestant use of the confessional. One of the great contributions to the church which was made by Protestants was to free the sacrament of confession from the confessional booth. Unfortunately, present-day Protestants have neglected confession almost entirely, and into the vacuum has come pastoral discourse. But Post-Reformation Protestants often made better use of the confessional than did Roman Catholics. The Roman church, unfortunately, made confession rigid and confined to the confessional booth. The Lutherans took the first step by declaring that a specific enumeration of sins was unnecessary for an adequate confession, thereby freeing the individual so that he might take to his priest those problems which were causing him the most trouble, concern, and anxiety. Puritan casuistry freed the clergyman from the necessity of pronouncing the absolution formula, thereby making the entire process even less formal.

The minister, to be sure, gave assurance of God's pardon, but now he could hear confessions in the parlor, kitchen, or when talking to a parishioner over the barnyard fence, and give a verbal but informal assurance of forgiveness. When Richard Baxter, the great Puritan divine, called upon the thousand families in his parish he knew why he called and so did his parishioners. He came to diagnose their spiritual state, offer forgiveness where needed and prescribe, admonish, and instruct. This is a far cry from the modern pastor who talks about the weather and almost everything else, in hope that being a hale fellow

The Catholic Priest

well met, at least a few might seek him out in time of trouble. Now the informality which was so hard won is again being lost as parishioners are required to make appointments with the church secretary to see the pastor in his study. As a result the number of people receiving pastoral counseling has declined even more.

Liberal theology has undoubtedly been responsible for discarding much of the pastor's authority and the sacramental emphasis of the past. Granted that the authority was often abused, and that sacramentalism in many denominations had lost its appeal and sometimes its intellectual integrity; but again we have an example of a religious household throwing out too much. To use the trite but apt phrase, "They have thrown out the baby with the bath water." Catholics were fortunately spared much of this until Vatican II. Roman Catholic pastors were more often sought out as arbiters in marital problems and other disputes than as counselors. But at least they were consulted. The use of the Sacrament of Confession has declined a great deal since Vatican II and the new liturgy lacks much of the appeal of the Tridentine Mass. Again the Old Catholic Movement is untouched by this and in many areas of the country is drawing fallen away Catholics who miss the old liturgy and the traditional faith of the catholic Church.

The priest is called to administer the sacraments and therefore he also has the responsibility of seeing that they are understood. Confession, or as it is now called in the Roman Church, the Sacrament of Reconciliation, offers more for the peace of soul and mind than anything that secular counselors can offer. Pastors need to integrate the teachings about the sacraments with their preaching program. It is another part of the command to go forth and preach the gospel to all nations. The gospel not only enlightens and teaches, but above all it brings men and women to be reconciled to God and to participate with Him in the Sacrament of the Holy Mass.

PART TWO
TRAINING

V.

THE PRIEST AS PREACHER

Luke **9:60** *Jesus said unto him, Let the dead bury the dead; but go thou and preach the Kingdom of God*

    The text from Luke should delight the heart of any fundamentalist, for Jesus refused to accept the excuse of a man who would put his father ahead of his call to preach the gospel. In many communities, particularly in the south, the pastor is most often called the preacher. I had a friend in the mountains of Pennsylvania who was most often called by the children the "**peacher**". Preaching was his principle function, and though he was only called upon to preach a few times a week, it overshadowed all his other duties. Of course, I am using the word preach in a very narrow sense. In a broader sense it includes not only the formal presentation from the pulpit but also the public demonstration of our actions. Preaching can be done through quiet conversation as well as dramatic oratory, from the pulpit or behind a lectern. To many Protestants a pastor is measured primarily by his role as preacher, and the pulpit is the central focus of every worship service.

    Preaching is important and in this we all agree. We may differ on other pastoral functions, but everyone agrees a pastor is called to preach the gospel. Seminaries and Bible Schools spend many hours attempting to train preachers. Such matters as delivery, voice projection, and in some schools, preparation, are a large part of the pastor's formal schooling. There is no particular right way to deliver a sermon, although, I suspect there are more wrong ways than I can imagine. What is fundamental is that the gospel be preached, and every church and every preacher claims to preach the gospel. Some even claim that only they preach the gospel and all other preachers fail to do so. It is not surprising that differences arise and we must understand why.

Bishop Karl Prüter

Much of the difficulty arises from our different beliefs about authority for our faith. When a Baptist minister sits down to prepare his sermon, he goes to the Bible. That is his source of all religious truth. Down the street at a more charismatic church the preacher may say, "I never prepare a sermon because when I get into the pulpit the Holy Spirit will tell me what to say." The fact is that the root cause of most religious differences lies in the fact that we have different sources for religious authority. Ask the average Baptist and he will say that the Bible is his source of truth. Ask the Unitarian and he will say, "reason." Ask the Lutheran and he will say, "Christ." Ask the Pentecostal and he will say "the Holy Spirit." Ask the Roman Catholic and he will say, "the Church." Ask the Methodist and he will say "experience with Christ." It is as if something occurred outside of your home and all the members of the family went to see it from a different window. They each would see the event from a different angle and therefore see it differently.

God manifests Himself in many ways. He has given us the Scriptures and they are for our instruction. He has given us minds and he expects us to use them. He has given us His Son so that we might learn from His example and through His Presence at Holy Mass. He has promised us His Holy Spirit that we might be led through life's many mazes. We are allowed to experience Him as we live our lives. And we have not only our own experience but the experiences of the saints and those with whom we walk in fellowship in the Body of Christ, the Holy Church. Each way is for our instruction. Each window brings in new light.

A good pastor who is determined to preach God's Word is open to every source of truth and utilizes them all. A good program, one which I have myself tried to follow is to read the Gospel and Epistle lesson for the coming Sunday on the previous Monday. And, of course, study it. Then during the week as I make my rounds I seek further light from the Holy Spirit and from the presence of Christ at daily Mass. One of the important sources of faith is the Church's two-thousand-year experience with God. But the Church has many levels. We are part of a local parish or congregation, part of a particular branch of the church which has dioceses, synods, conferences, associations, etc. When such groups meet the participants always invoke the Holy Spirit, although they don't always heed Him. Finally, the Universal Church occasionally convokes councils of its hierarchy. The bishop, presumably, is the repository of the faith for the diocese which he serves. But in preparing sermons it is the local congregation or parish that is most relevant. The pastor needs to make regular parish calls, first, so that he might know the needs of his parishioners, and secondly, so that through them he might receive further direction in the preparation of his sermon. For Christ is truly the head of the Church and He seeks to direct His Church, not only through the bishop and pastors, but through every single member of the Church. It is important that the members pray for their pastor and that he pray for them. Only in this way can they support one another in the Christian life. I look upon sermon preparation in the same way as someone going into a garden to gather food. I not only learn about some of the needs of the parishioners that need to be addressed from the pulpit, but through their prayers and their fellowship with Christ, I gather the experiences of the lives and find the words needed to share my vision with them in the coming Sunday sermon. Many pastors share their experiences with Christ, their inspiration in prayer, or their victories over adversity, and thereby they separate themselves from the congregation. We are all part of this life together, and the sermon must be the sum total of our experiences and the revelation of Christ through us.

The first reason for involving the parish in sermon preparation is that this is the way it is supposed to be done. But many pastors are amazed to discover that people are quick to judge them and seem delighted when they make mistakes. The reason is obvious: their sermons and every sermon are a judgment. When you preach that this is the way we should live, you are saying, indirectly, that the way we live is less than perfect. You are telling the congregation that they must improve. And the reaction that is apt to pop into their minds is, "Well you are not so hot yourself." This is another reason why the sermon should be inclusive and the product of the entire congregation. The pastor doesn't have to tell them. The congregation very quickly senses this. But he probably should share with them and remind them that his sermons are the result of their cooperative effort. But above all, no priest should rely upon any one source of religious truth. God expects us to use every gift he has given us, the Bible, our minds, our experiences, the Church, His inestimable gift of his Son Jesus Christ and the Holy Spirit.

Further, Christ expects the priest, the Church expects him, the bishop expects him, and the parish expects him, to be a visible sermon for the gospel. One reason why he is required to wear clericals is to increase his visibility. If he is needed he can readily be seen, but more importantly he is the gospel made visible. If you see a priest misbehaving think of him as a poor sermon. And if he gives too many poor sermons both in the pulpit and/or on the street, it is up to the bishop to remove him.

Finally, the pastor of the church is expected to give, at least one full working day to sermon preparation. In the past Catholic priests probably spent less, but the church is increasingly aware of the fact that today's congregations expect more from the pastors as preachers than they did prior to Vatican II. With the decline in the number of priests, the remaining priests have to carry an increased work load, and finding a full day for the sermon may be difficult. The church has sought to involve the laity and the diaconate more to provide help for the busy pastor. A pastor who is too busy to properly prepare himself to preach the gospel needs to reassess and reorient his priorities. Two things are primary to a priestly vocation: that the priest properly preach the gospel, and that he properly administer the sacraments.

VI.
THE ROLE OF THE PRIEST AT WEDDINGS

I spent a lot of time recently reading Roman Catholic Canon law regarding marriage. I came away with two perspectives. First, that at the wedding ceremony the role of the priest is minimal. His task is to assist at the wedding. Nothing more or less. In fact, he is not even necessary because under special circumstances a layman can be appointed to fill this role (Roman Catholic Canon #1112).

Popular opinion believes that the priest is important to the ceremony, and not important in what must precede the celebration of marriage, or to the couple's life after the wedding. Only a lovesick bride and groom and their parents allow the ceremony to eclipse reality. In the marriage service the couple vow before God to bind themselves together in love. As a couple they pledge to serve Him and to live according to His Holy Laws. They also have gathered the parish together that they may share their vows and witness with those among whom they will live. For if they are planning to live a Christian life together, and they say that they are, it follows that they will live in community with the members of their parish church.

This is why it is important that the wedding take place in the parish church. The couple may not always live in the parish in which the wedding takes place, but it is here they pledge their vows, and if they move on they will transfer their membership and their vows to a new parish of the People of God. In the entire process the assumption is made that the newly married couple will live a life within the Church. When they call at the rectory to arrange for the wedding, they will be asked to produce baptismal and confirmation certificates. If they come from another parish the priest there will be contacted to make certain there are no impediments to the marriage. Then the banns will be announced for the three Sundays prior to the wedding. Again there is the assumption that they are known in the parish and the people are well acquainted with the details of their lives. The banns read as follows:

> *N. N. and N. N. propose to enter into the Holy Estate of matrimony according to God's ordinance. They desire that prayer be made for them, that they may be prospered in it. If any one can show just cause why they may not be joined together, I exhort him to make known such objection before the day of marriage.*

The priest must counsel the couple before the marriage, pointing out its sacredness as well as its hazards and pitfalls. I also feel it important to help the couple come down from cloud 9 and to discuss some very mundane details. I have had couples come to me where the bride did not know how much the groom earned, even though they planned to live on one income. Goals need to be discussed, if not set, before the marriage takes place, and a good pastoral counselor can help the couple see what marriage to one another will be like. Of course, he cannot refuse to assist at the wedding because he doesn't think they are right for each other, or even because he feels that the marriage won't work. (I'll admit that I have been tempted many times!) On the other hand, he doesn't run a wedding chapel either, and for better or for worse these are people from his parish, and the parish, like the couple, may be stuck with a bad marriage. The priest and the parish are expected to furnish the Christian couple assistance to support the matrimonial estate. The canons require the priest to give support in many ways.

He tries to strengthen Christian marriage in his parish by giving instruction through his homilies and through catechism instruction to children, young people, and adults. The canons even require that he avail himself of the media to get across to the entire community the basis and principles of sound marriage.

Nor has the task been left entirely to the pastor. The priest does have the duty of giving premarital counseling, but the church has put into place a variety of educational programs, including Cana classes and marriage encounter programs. Ideally, of course, the parochial school, where it still exists, is the best vehicle for ongoing family education.

The Catholic Priest

It is hard to describe the liturgical celebration of marriage as anything else but a clarifying experience that the spouses share in the mystery and the unity and love that exists between Christ and His Church. Even as they are one person, so are we all one in Christ's Body, His Holy Catholic Church. So well has the Church conveyed this message that many Catholics who get a divorce simultaneously divorce themselves from the Church. They do so not because the Church opposes divorce, or in some cases denies them the Sacrament, but because they feel their ties are broken with their spouse and consequently also with the Church. We know from experience that when a couple separates, it becomes difficult in most cases for even one party to continue a relationship with friends they previously shared. The pastor here is also in a dilemma. It is important that both parties continue their relationship in the parish church. First, because it is in itself important. Secondly, more than ever they need the support of the parish and friends. In some cases it might be easier if one or the other chose another parish and there received the support of the members and of the Sacrament. But which party should make the change is a question to challenge Solomon.

Fortunately, even in this day of easy divorce, marriages that take place within the church do stand up. In part, it may be due to the parishes that are ready to assist couples in trouble with prayers, their counsel, the pastor's assistance, the Sacraments, and in many cases material support when marriages are in difficulty due to financial hard times. The parish must have a discretionary fund at the pastor's disposal so that he may be able to give help in critical situations.

It is not that there are no other agencies besides the parish which can assist, but that this is a primary responsibility of the Church. In addition, the Church is one of the few agencies that can provide support quietly and confidentially. A trip to the welfare office is noticed, while a trip to the pastor's study could occur for any number of reasons. The church needs to be available in times of trouble.

I am concerned by the number of psychologists who have gone into grief counseling as their latest specialty, and by the number of support groups for people with catastrophic diseases or loved ones suffering from such illnesses. I don't know what it tells you, but it tells me that the Church is not doing its job. If the Church is doing its job in these areas than we have failed to get out the message.

I once had a parish in New Hampshire, and in my first year I had four funerals for suicides. I tried to figure out why in a town of seven hundred people there should be that many suicides in a single year. I soon realized that there were many lonely people who never had anyone call upon them or even had a neighbor they could talk with. A good number of them were in the lumber industry, and lived in little shacks apart from neighbors, with their nearest relatives in towns hundreds of miles away. My predecessor had never called on these people although he often denounced their life style from the pulpit. I resolved to call on every home in the town at least once a year, and obviously where I saw the need, I called as often as it took to meet their needs. This is what the canons mean when they say the pastor must continue the assistance he gave at the wedding throughout the marriage. While I had not married any of the folk in the town, they too, had a claim upon my services simply because they were children of God. A priest is responsible for the physical, mental, and spiritual well-being of everyone who resides in his parish. And, more importantly, the entire congregation, the whole Church, must be involved.

This is not easy! In my first parish I quickly learned how hard it is to involve the whole parish, in a town where "foreigners" were customarily ostracized (a foreigner being defined as someone who had come from another town). Since some of the latter had lived there for over forty years one can understand why they felt bitter at being looked upon as outsiders. Such people often become so bitter they were beyond help. I once went to a concerned lady in the parish and asked her to call on a lady who had complained to me that in the eight years she had lived in the community no one had made friends with her. She was terribly lonely and wanted nothing more than companionship. But when my would-be Good Samaritan called she was almost thrown out of the house. The woman said that no one had bothered to talk to her in eight years and she could get along quite well by herself, "Thank you very much."

Yes, we get occasional rebuffs, but if we care enough we continue trying. And, of course, if the parish had been doing its job there never would have been an eight-year lapse. But people often do not realize how the accepted life style of a community affects different individuals. That's what the church and the pastors are for. A good priest will do much to raise the consciousness of the community. A pastor often has to be the conscience of the community. He doesn't preach sermons on sobriety to a congregation of teetotalers, but he preaches about the more common sins of gossip, indifference to our neighbors' needs, and the petty jealousies and hatreds that separate us from God and neighbor.

I seem to have gotten away from the priest's role in marriage, but I assure you that I haven't. Everything we do in the church is integrated into the whole. Both priest and laity when they go to a wedding need to weigh with reverent minds what the Lord teaches concerning marriage and their role. It is not a superficial role which is played, but the taking on of a serious and life-long responsibility. Admittedly, we sometimes fall far short of giving this kind of support, but by canon law this is what the priest is required to give.

VII.

THE PRIEST AS MISSIONARY

Every clergyman knows that he is called to be a missionary. The words of Jesus are very clear, "Go ye into all the world, and preach the gospel to the whole creation" (*Mark* 16:5). It would seem that there would be no great differences in the approach to missionary work between Catholics and Protestants, but William Orchard has pointed out a very fundamental difference. Protestant Churches, particularly those in Europe, are often state churches or, at least, maintain a strong national identity. For examples, see the Church of England, etc.

But the Church of Jesus Christ is and always has been universal. When He sent His disciples into the WHOLE world He made a slight break with Jewish tradition. There had always been proselytes, but never before had Jews gone out to share the gospel so freely with so many. Paul very aggresively went out among the Gentiles and said, "There cannot be Greek and Jew, circumcision and uncircumcision, barbarian, Scythian, bondman, freeman; but Christ is all, and in all." And again in *Revelation* John tells us, "Behold, a great multitude, which no man could number, out of every nation, and of all tribes and peoples and tongues" (*Rev.* 7:9). It was William Orchard who noted that the Reformation had not only failed to heal the division of the Church, but had actually made the situation worse. If the aim of the reformers was to restore the New Testament Church then they should first have healed the division between East and West. Having failed to do so, they cannot claim to have recreated the Church as Christ intended.

What they did was to divide the Church further along national lines. Each king or prince determined whether the church in his state would be Catholic or Protestant. In England every child born in that country was automatically a member of the Church of England. Thus the Church became further removed from what Christ intended. The Roman Church continued to claim that it was the One Undivided

Church, but no objective observer believed her claim. The church was now shattered as never before. Further compounding the error was the attitude that regarded the situation as necessary and right. First, each religious group felt it was separating itself from unbelievers, but secondly there arose a feeling which in many cases caused Christians to refuse to evangelize among unbelievers.

Let me illustrate what has happened and is happening. First there is a national or cultural exclusion of people. When I was in seminary, in the third year each student was required to serve as a student assistant pastor at some parish. I was assigned to All Saints Lutheran Church in Philadelphia. It was an old church and one in which the membership was declining. The pastor's explanation for the declining membership was that the people were moving out of the neighborhood. What he failed to observe was that every time one of his member families moved out, another family (or often two families) moved into the house that the members had vacated. What was unsaid was the fact that the member family had either been of German or Scandinavian origin and the new family or families were either Irish or Italian. And as everyone knows if you are Irish or Italian you are Roman Catholic and destined to remain so until you die. The pastor never called twice upon a family who on the first call said they were Catholic, even though it was often obvious that they didn't work very hard at being Catholic. In the pastor's mind, if you were Irish or Italian you were not good prospects for the Lutheran Church.

In my first parish after leaving seminary, I served a New England Yankee congregation in Maine. When I began to bring in French Canadians as members, I detected immediate hostility. They were French and so were, and should ever remain, Roman Catholic. I know many ethnic churches that freeze out anyone in the neighborhood not of their ethnic origin who would presume to attend their church.

A Catholic priest thinks of himself first as a servant of the "catholic," that is the "universal," Church. He often recruits people from every ethnic background simply because the Church he serves claims to be universal. Again, it is not a perfect system. In fact, Rome has organized in America thousands of so-called "ethnic" parishes. But they often came about because the pastor of an Italian parish, for example, gathered in many Poles, and when the two groups did not get along, the parish was divided along more agreeable lines. *But both the pastor and the bishop, who did the dividing, believed there was room in*

The Catholic Priest

the One Holy Catholic and Apostolic church for both Poles and Italians (even though both of them were probably Irish!).

A second division is often along class lines. We often think of certain denominations, such as small Pentecostal Churches, as being made up of poor people, or in the case of the Episcopalians and the Presbyterians, as having wealthy parishioners. In Chicago we shared our facilities with an Anglican group, and my friend, the pastor of the Anglican Church, often took charge of our bookstore and chapel while I worked at a secular job. The good father upset me no end when I discovered that he only welcomed those into the store who were reasonably well dressed and seemed to be of a certain class. The homeless, the jobless and even the working poor were not welcomed. Again, Catholic Churches as a whole enjoy a wider social spectrum.

This is not to say there are not Catholic parishes which can be regarded as rich and others as poor. But this has more to do with the neighborhoods in which these churches are located. Prior to Vatican II every Catholic was expected to attend the church in his own neighborhood. The only good reason that he might have to transfer to a different parish is if he wished to go to a church of a different rite. The priest, again, is at an advantage when he does missionary work. The Church he serves is Catholic, that is universal, and hence he may seek to convert rich and poor alike.

A friend of mine was once pastor of a Protestant Church on Nantucket Island. The people who attended had money which their ancestors had acquired in the fishing industry. He referred to his parishioners as "codfish aristocrats." At the first meeting of his board of deacons they read the minutes of the last meeting and decided there was no new business and they considered adjournment. My friend asked if there weren't any poor in the church who were in need and was told by one deacon, "Oh we wouldn't have any of those people in the church." It follows that the church in the past must have had pastors who shared this sentiment, but for a Catholic priest it would be almost impossible because he always thinks of himself as a pastor in the One Holy Catholic and Universal Church. It is the Church of ALL people.

The final division in the Church is a great paradox. Let me illustrate it in this way. If a new family moves into the community where I live, the churches here will be much interested. If it is found that they are Presbyterian, the pastors of all the churches will show great interest. There is no Presbyterian church here and the Church of

Christ, The Baptist, and the Assembly of God pastors will all make numerous calls and perhaps in due time the family will go to one or the other of these three local churches. But, if the family is what I call "a birthright unbeliever," that is someone who has no religious affiliation, the pastors may make one call but it will be the last. You may well ask, "Why? Is this not the kind of person for whom the churches express so much concern?" After all, when revivals are held is not their purpose to win people to Christ? But are the birthright unbelievers urged to come to revivals? Oh, someone may drop a leaflet at their door, but in the weeks of preparation for the revival, the pastor at whose church it will take place calls upon the uncommitted Presbyterians, Methodists, *et al.*

He does so because it is in his self interest to do so. He is expected to build up the congregation, that is, to increase its membership. He will probably only be in this parish three to five years and if he is going to build membership he is more likely to do so by calling upon lukewarm members of other denominations than by calling upon birthright unbelievers. To win someone from the latter group will take years, more years than the pastor may intend to stay in the community. I contend that almost no one calls upon these people to win them to Christ. I have known many Catholic priests and have yet to meet one who felt under pressure to increase the membership of the parish church. When he is assigned to a parish, the bishop tells him he is responsible for everyone in the parish, Catholic, Protestant, and birthright unbelievers. He is a missionary to all who are not Catholic. He is the pre-eminent sheepstealer. If they are outside of the Catholic Church, he needs to pray for them and to seek to convert them to the One Holy Catholic and Apostolic Church.

Prior to Vatican II the Roman Catholic Church held itself aloof from other Christian Churches. But it always thought of them as Christian, albeit separated, brethren. Separated Brethren isn't a bad term. It sure beats "the Whore of Babylon," a term by which some Protestants describe the Roman Church. A great contradiction in the Protestant missionary enterprise is that while Protestant pastors may not seek to bring in Blacks to the local church, Africa is crawling with the missionaries of these same churches, of every description. And while many churches are willing to bless the Black converts, it is rather like a scene from *The Fiddler on the Roof*, where the people ask the rabbi if there is a blessing for the Czar. He is taken aback, and then without

The Catholic Priest

further preamble he comes up with a suitable blessing. "May the Lord bless him and keep him—far far away from us." The result of the missionary work has not been to build a universal church but to fragment the Church even further. Whatever Protestantism may claim, it falls short of being the Universal Church.

Even the Roman Church, although it is found in most areas of the world, cannot make a credible claim to universality. It is a problem all Christians face. It affects our churches and it even affects the sacraments. The Scriptures may speak of One Baptism but few churches accept this teaching. However, when Lutherans, Baptists, or Episcopalians join the Roman Catholic Church they are not rebaptized. The priest recognizes not only that the Church itself should be universal, but that the Sacrament of Baptism by which we are admitted into the Church is also universal.

The Catholic priest, like all Christian clergymen, is a missionary because of Christ's command that we are to go forth and preach to the whole world. Traditionally, he has performed this task in several different ways. Most Catholic Churches during this century have held "inquiry" classes, or classes of instruction, for people who during the year have indicated an interest in the Catholic faith. When there are enough people to form a class the pastor announces it from the pulpit, by mail, by a sign on the side of the church, and/or in newspaper advertisements. The classes deal with the teachings of the church, its practices, its history, and how it compares to other denominations and even non-Christian faiths. After the course is over those who have attended are asked if they wish to become members of the Catholic Church. Other Catholic approaches to evangelism include home study courses sponsored by the Knights of Columbus. Once the course is completed, those who are interested in entering the Church will be directed to the Catholic parish and to the priest nearest to the student's home.

The Catholic Church has made very little use of the media. A number of years ago Bishop Fulton Sheen had a very successful television program, but after his program ended, the Church virtually dropped out of television and radio programming. I can't tell you why, but I can make a guess. As a missionary tool it is just not very effective. The huge Protestant programs *have* brought in billions of dollars for the programmer—but very few souls for Christ. (The one program that seems most sincere in its attempt to win souls is the Reverend Billy Graham's *Hour of Decision*.) Have you ever met even one active

Christian who was formerly a birthright unbeliever, and who was won over to Christ through a television or radio program? These programs may be spectacular to view, but they are not very good tools for the true evangelist or the missionary.

The one modern tool that has proven effective, but has largely been overlooked by both Protestants and Catholics, is the telephone. Many churches are beginning to try it and it works. It works because it puts the missionary on a one-to-one basis with someone who may have a particular need. Missionary work has been properly defined as one thirsty man telling another thirsty man where he can find water. In this approach the parish priest can participate either personally, or by organizing a group of laity to help him in this missionary effort.

But whatever the medium, the message must be clear. It must be a call to accept Christ and His Universal Church. The appeal to unbelievers must never be, "We invite you to come to St. John's Church because it is made up of Irish-Americans who want to have an Irish parish." Or, "We are a group of suburbanites, who feel a church made up of people like us would help provide the community with a central place for religious and social activities." That sort of "evangelizing" often means a lot of social activities with very little religion. The Catholic priest must never build a parish on any foundation except the Rock which is Christ. Nor may the Church be anything but universal. No flag should ever be flown in the chancel until we have a flag for the Kingdom of God.

One of the fastest growing churches of this century was Bishop Carfora's Old Roman Catholic Church. It rose like a meteor by gathering Catholics into ethnic parishes, i.e., Ukrainian, Italian, Lithuanian, etc., and it fell apart within two decades because of its divisiveness. A church which is German or Irish, Baptist or Methodist, Roman Catholic or Orthodox, cannot claim to be the Church which Jesus gave us. It must first of all be Universal, and second it must be Catholic, Orthodox, Apostolic, and Evangelical. We all have the same history and running through our doctrines are all these elements regardless of what the signboard in front of the church says. It has been said that no person is exclusively male or female but we are all a bit of both. How much more true is it that no Catholic can deny his Evangelical roots and no Evangelical can deny his Catholic roots. The priest as missionary needs to keep before his parish and community the universality of the Church. Christ did not die for some of us, but for all.

VIII.
THE PRIEST AS HEALER

It is obvious that the priest is called to be something more than a preacher and a teacher. Jesus in His ministry went about teaching and healing. The healing function of the priest and the Church has often been forgotten or neglected. Prior to the Reformation the priest was often not only the principle healer in the community but often the only healer. At the best the healing arts of the day as provided by physicians were quite primitive. Prayer and the patient's own inner resources were the first line of defense against disease or injury. When a person was ill, the priest was notified so that he might offer prayer at the altar and visit the patient and offer the consolations of the Church. These included prayer, anointing with oil, and bringing the Blessed Sacrament so that the patient might, even when bed-ridden, still feel a part of the on-going life of the parish.

In addition, it was the Church that provided the hospitals and the education for the physicians. It also provided special healing services such as on St. Blaise's Day (February 3) when those who suffered from throat ailments were urged to come to the church that their throats might be blessed and through prayer healed. Chapels were set aside in many parts of the world so that people could come and pray for healing.

The Reformation did not do away with all of the healing ministry, for many of the Protestant Churches retained Catholic practices. Prayer at the altar, prayer at the bedside, the founding of hospitals, and even the anointing with oil, were retained by some Protestant Churches, most notably the Lutherans and the Church of England. Special shrines for healing and special holy days, such as St. Blaise's Day, were discarded by most of Protestantism as being pagan or superstitious.

With the advent of modern medicine the role of the church in healing was notably lessened. In fact, much of it was forgotten and even where it was remembered its importance was reduced to the statement, "Well, I guess, now all we can do is pray." When all else fails we resort to prayer. Prayer for many is no longer the first defense against disease, and cynics will say we should note how much healthier the population is as a result. The comment fails to take into account that prayer works hand-in-hand with other types of therapy.

It is also overlooked that healing must be holistic. We should seek to be truly whole and healthy, not only physically, but also mentally and spiritually. Who dares to say that modern medical miracles have done much for man's mental and spiritual health? The numbers who resort to drugs as an escape cry aloud for the healing that the Christ alone can offer. A truth known to every psychiatrist, when dealing with the guilt-ridden, is that only a priest can offer a remedy. Through the confessional millions have found the only relief that can be offered to many troubled souls, the mercy and forgiveness of God.

The failure of Protestantism to continue the healing ministry of Christ resulted in the rise of Christian Science as a distinct sect which placed its main emphasis on healing. It also opened the door to so-called fundamentalist faith healers. Neither of these doctrines places healing within the framework of the whole gospel. The healing role of the Catholic priest is often overlooked precisely because it is only a small portion of the gospel which he has to present to the world. Christ, after all, was a healer Himself, but He was much more than that. He came to bring life abundant and life eternal. This is the gospel the priest must offer to the world. Daily, he goes before the altar of God to offer the Holy Mass and to preach the gospel. In the Mass there is the commemoration of the living, and it is here that he brings before God the needs of his parishioners. He prays for the sick of body, mind, and soul. He prays for the prisoners, and for any special needs which his parishioners may have. He prays for the sick, because he is required to do so as a Christian and because of his calling. In addition, when he mentions these needs at the Mass, it reminds the congregation that they too should offer prayers for their fellow parishioners and neighbors. We pray not alone but as members of Christ's Body, the Holy Catholic Church.

Christ instructed us to pray for the prisoners and the priest does so, first, because the prisoner is surely in need of prayer. But the public prayer is also a public announcement that we are concerned for the prisoner and that he is one among us. I am certain that if someone, in many churches I can think of, were arrested and the pastor offered

The Catholic Priest

prayer for him, some of the members would be scandalized, preferring to shun the prisoner and treat him as a publican and a sinner.

After the Mass, the priest will begin to schedule his calls to those who are sick either in the hospital or at home. For this he needs the help of the members of the congregation. When they go to the hospital they need to notify their priest. They need also to tell him, from time to time, about neighbors and other parishioners who are hospitalized. He needs to make preparation for his calls. Before he leaves the rectory he should pray for those he is to call upon and be prepared to let the Holy Spirit show him how he can best meet their needs. When he comes to the hospital he must be prepared to listen to the concerns of the parishioner. He may be asked to hear his confession and to bring him the Blessed Sacrament. In any case, before he leaves, he will offer prayer and sometimes the rite of anointing with oil. The calls should never be routine. The priest must assess each situation and be ready to offer whatever is necessary. Also as he makes his call, he will often meet relatives of the one who is ill, and he must be prepared to meet their needs as well. Often they are extremely concerned and fearful and have need for both prayer and counseling. No matter how busy the priest is and no matter how many more calls he must make he must take time to serve not only the sick, but their loved ones as well.

The priest must always inform his parishioners that he is available to them twenty-four hours a day. It seems very generous and it is, but in forty-six years in the ministry I have never had anyone abuse this privilege. I have had some difficult nights, however. I remember once being called at one in the morning to come to a hospital because the three year old son of one of my parishioners had died. The hospital was twenty minutes away and I prayed during every one of those minutes. I was sure that if I were to say any words of comfort to the bereaved parents the Holy Spirit would have to give them to me. I didn't know how difficult the situation was until I entered the hospital room where the parents were, together with the mother's sister and brother-in-law, the doctor, an undertaker, and a nurse. As soon as I was introduced everyone fled, leaving me with the parents. There we were, the four of us, the parents, me, and the Holy Spirit. I do not know what I said or what prayer I offered, but looking back I realize that nothing I said mattered so much as the fact that I, God's human representative, was there. They didn't understand why their child died, but they were glad that the God who gave them the child cared enough to send His emissary in their time of trial.

A few years earlier, in a parish in New Hampshire, news was brought to me that the wife of one of my parishioners had committed suicide. I immediately drove out to their home and found dozens of cars in the yard. The sheriff was there, the coroner, a doctor, and several other officials. The husband came to me as I got out of my car and walked up the drive. We talked for a bit and again I can't recall what I said, but like the later incident I had prayed every minute while I was on the way. I prayed again when it was time to prepare the funeral sermon and again when I called upon the husband a few days after the funeral. I remember not what I said to him, but what he said to me. He said, "You can't have any idea how I felt surrounded by dozens of people who had all kind of questions for me that I wasn't in any condition to answer. I felt my world falling apart and then I saw that white clerical collar and you walking up the drive. That was all the help I needed." Again I was fairly new in the parish and it wasn't me he was happy to see, but the white clerical collar, a symbol that the wearer was God's servant. These are not easy occasions for the priest, but they are the occasions that make his calling worthwhile.

Looking back over the years, I find that it is at times of bereavement that I feel best about my calling. Not only because through my ministry I am able to bring consolation to many, but also because at these times many of the bereaved begin for the first time in years to reassess their lives. It is a time when the priest has to employ his skills as a healer. First, the bereaved always feels a burden of guilt. If the mother has died, the child feels guilty because he feels he had not done enough for the mother.

Sometimes the bereaved may even feel responsible for the parent's death. The worst incident I ever experienced was when a woman, whom I had not known well, called me at her husband's death. It seemed that the day before the insurance man had come to collect her husband's insurance premium. As she went to get her purse to get the premium money she remarked to her husband in a joking manner, "How come I have to pay on this every month and I never get to collect?" Believe me, she was having trouble coping with her guilt. I answered with logic by saying, "We all make remarks like this all the time." After the funeral it took many calls to help her through that situation.

The Catholic Priest

The funeral service of the Church fortunately provides Scriptures that help the bereaved deal with their guilt, both real and imaginary. When I was in the North Berwyn parish I had more than twenty funerals a year, of which about eighteen were for families I had not previously known. Usually about three or four would seriously begin to think about their relationship with God, and soon asked about becoming members of the Church. God seems very close when someone is born into a family, and again, when someone in the family dies. Families who have heretofore had little to do with God need help in attempting to find a place for Him in their lives. At a death they feel, perhaps for the first time, a need for Him. Further, they now have problems which they know are too large for them to handle without God. The priest has to be a therapist here, and carefully serve to introduce these people to that Person Who has been a stranger to them, namely, God. It is a difficult but exciting time for both the bereaved and the priest. In this situation there are often no guidelines, and the priest must depend entirely on the Holy Spirit.

Today few Catholic Churches have frequent healing services although there is a Mass for the Sick. At this Mass there is provision for the anointing of any who are sick either of body, mind, or soul. The only problem is that the Mass is celebrated so infrequently. This is the priest's responsibility and the failure to do so on his part is a serious neglect of his duties as a healer.

One of the problems that pastors (both Catholic and Protestant) have is that people so casually ask them to pray for them. The pastors respond in an equally casual manner. It is almost as if neither party takes this responsibility seriously. When a priest is asked to pray for someone, he must, indeed, do so both in his private prayers and at the celebration of Mass. It is wise to let the party who requested prayer know that he has followed through and offered the requested prayers. Of course, in the Commemoration of the Living the names of those prayed for are often said aloud and it is a practice that makes prayer for the sick a communal concern.

So far we have spoken only of the priest's healing role in connection with his parish. But as Jesus pointed out there are other sheep that are not in the fold. When a priest visits a hospital he is frequently called upon to meet with Protestants, Jews, and even those of no faith at all. Here he must use tact and take the time to be informed concerning the practices of people outside the Catholic Church. One of my professors in seminary was asked to visit a lady in the hospital and was told she was of the same faith as he was, a Lutheran. He came to the bedside and introduced himself and asked if she would like to receive Holy Communion. Immediately, she became hysterical and began to scream. After awhile when she had calmed down a bit he learned that she came from Germany and where she lived the pastor never offered communion to the sick unless they were dying. Apparently she was not ready to go. We need to know something about the religious practices and culture of those to whom we presume to minister.

Granted that a Catholic priest must act according to the practices of his own church; he must also learn to be flexible. Obviously, if he is at the bedside of a Baptist and offers prayer he does not say the "Hail Mary." Further, although it is Catholic practice to end a prayer, "In the Name of the Father, the Son, and the Holy Spirit," most Protestants would be more comfortable with "In Jesus's Name we Pray." I know many will take issue with me regarding our ministry to people of Buddhist and Hindu faiths, and will say we must always be true to our calling and pray in the Name of Jesus. Regardless, I feel it would be perfectly proper to end a prayer with "In Thy Name. Amen," or simply with "Amen." Since we all believe in God can't we leave it at that? We should not choose the occasion of someone lying ill in a sick bed to begin to define "God" or to try to carry on a theological discussion. Jesus, as he went about healing and preaching, spoke to people of other beliefs and refused none. In their time of need He did not refuse the Samaritan woman, nor the Roman centurian; for He did, indeed, preach the gospel to all nations. And so a Catholic priest must do likewise, remembering that he is called as a preacher, teacher, and healer to serve all who have need of his services.

IX.

PREPARATION FOR THE HOLY AND PRIESTLY LIFE

In our first lesson we dealt with the call to the priesthood and with Holy Orders. But even as with Christ himself, when he had been baptized and the voice from Heaven proclaimed, "This is my beloved Son, in whom I am well pleased," anyone who receives such a call must consider what it means. Christ spent forty days and nights wrestling with this question and to consider what he must do to prepare himself for what He had been called to do.

For which of us, when we are called, are living fully the life to which Jesus calls us? Oh, we may have been moved at our Baptism or Confirmation to dedicate our life to Christ, but who has lived fully the life he intended to live? At the most we make some superficial changes in our life style. Some of these changes may even have been dramatic. A drunkard may have given up drinking, a philanderer may have become faithful to his or her spouse, and a thief may have turned to honest labor. But God expects something more. It is not enough that we do no evil, but He wants our love and our service as well. To live the Christian life means to become God-centered. It means to spend all of our days in service to Him.

Even our secular jobs can be dedicated to His service. The story is told of a man who came by and saw three men at work in the building of a great cathedral. He asked the first one what he was doing and the man replied, "I am hewing stone," Then he asked the second man what he was doing, and the worker replied, "I am earning ten dollars and hour." But when he asked the third man what he was doing, the response was, "*I am building a cathedral.*" Although all *seemed* to be doing exactly the same thing, one man clearly had a higher aim and felt his employer was neither the man who assigned him his task nor the man who paid his wages. He worked for God.

If it is true that we have all, at some time, dedicated our lives to God, why is it that there are so few lives that are completely absorbed in God? Why can so few honestly say that God is constantly in our thoughts, and that He is at all times first in our life? Why is it so few can say that, in all our decisions, we choose only those which we know are most pleasing to God?

Now I am aware that there are many Christians who would contend that it is not important that we live lives that are 100% dedicated to God. "For after all," they argue, "If we are saved we are already destined for heaven and additional 'good works' won't make any difference." Catholics have never contended that "good works" can "save" anyone, or even that living a good life can save anyone. What we do contend is that the saved, *because they are saved*, live good and holy lives and that those who don't live good lives obviously were never saved.

The next thought one might have is, of course, is it possible for anyone to live a life like Christ lived? If we believe in Christ and His words, it must be possible. Did He not invite us to follow Him, and did not the apostles admonish us all to live in Christ and receive into our hearts?

Christians often don't give this idea very serious consideration, though, because it is an overwhelming challenge. How does one go about living a life in Christ? The answer, as the Church teaches us, lies in prayer and discipline.

The act of prayer is simplicity itself. To be in prayer means simply to be in touch with Christ. We too often think of prayer as being only verbal. But just as when we are with other people on a one-to-one basis we are in communion with one another without feeling the necessity of talking every minute we are together, so, too, we can be in communion with the Lord without verbalizing it.

The second requirement, discipline, goes hand-in-hand with our prayer. How can we live a life of constant prayer? The monks and sisters in the church have managed it very well, through various *disciplines* which they have developed over the centuries. Being disciplined, like taking part in prayer, can also be very simple. Think of another word for discipline as "organization." I myself don't care for the term because I am often overwhelmed by my lack of organization. I can accept that—but I don't like thinking of myself of being undisciplined!

The Catholic Priest

A disciplined religious life is no different than any other kind of structured existence. Discipline involves four basic items: setting of goals, establishing priorities, setting aside time, and attention to necessary details. We set our primary goal when we made our initial commitment to Christ at our baptism or confirmation. We vowed then that we would live our life in Him, and that in all our doings, both religious and secular, we would be guided by the Holy Spirit.

This commitment calls first of all for a disciplined use of our time. The monks and the cloistered sisters were able to give a lot of thought to the ritual of daily disciplines. In the monstery they divided the day into nine *canonical* hours, which were times set aside for prayers. Many began with Matins at 2 A.M. and ended with compline at 10 P.M. Hardly a schedule that the rest of us would be willing to keep. But let's look at what they accomplished and how we might adapt their ideas about time to our own daily lives.

First, they began the day with a simple prayer that has served Christians for a very long time. I like it and try to say it at the beginning of each day. It goes like this:

> *O Lord, our heavenly Father, Almighty and Everlasting God, who hast safely brought us to the beginning of this day: defend us in the same with thy mighty power and grant that this day we fall into no sin, neither run into any kind of danger; but that all our doings, being ordered by thy governance, may be righteous in thy sight; through Jesus Christ, our Lord. Amen.*

But it is not enough just to say it. If you say it, *you have asked that God be with you throughout the day.* If so, during the day you must acknowlege His presence from time to time. Thomas à Kempis called it the "practice of the presence of God." Of course, we acknowledge Him at meal times when we take a moment to offer thanks, but our times of acknowledgment are all too few. Europeans a decade ago were very fortunate. They had a three-hour dinner period at noon. It meant that anyone who wanted to go to Mass at that time could—and a great many did. In small towns where there was no Mass at noon the churches were open for any who wished to drop in for prayer. Also the hillsides were dotted with small chapels and wayside shrines and those going to or from the fields could stop for a moment of prayer.

The daily Mass, for the priest, is an essential part of his discipline. At least once a day he is able to experience Christ in the most intimate way known to man, by sharing a meal at the Lord's Table. Prior to Vatican II, a priest was required to say the Breviary daily. This was a long and complicated series of Bible readings and prayers which took anywhere from one to two hours if followed conscientiously. After Vatican II it was no longer mandatory to say the Breviary, although it was assumed that most priests would continue this rite or substitute an equally rigorous ceremony in its place. Unfortunately, many priests did not have the self discipline required, and one of the predictable results was the exodus of thousands of priests from the Church. There were other reasons as well, but in my opinion this was the single most important one. Without a disciplined devotional life it becomes all too easy to lose the faith.

It goes without saying then that one should not end the day without a closing prayer, and an assessment of the day and one's personal relationship with God. The early Pilgrims and Puritans who came to America had a practice of keeping a daily record. I hesitate to say "diary," because it was more like an account book, since they truly felt that God held them accountable for their actions.

It doesn't matter a great deal what form your own personal discipline takes—but it does matter that you have one. It may consist simply of the morning prayer. Many Catholics begin the day by making the sign of the cross "In the Name of the Father, and of the Son, and of the Holy Spirit. Amen." At meals they say grace, in the evening they may read the Bible, and before bedtime say another prayer.

For a long time my wife and I started the day with a devotional reading followed by the Litany for Peace. For the devotional reading we used *The Imitation of Christ*, *Poustinia*, Father Orchard's prayer book called *The Temple*, and Grou's *Spiritual Maxims*. We also read Orchard's book on simplicity. I feel very fortunate in having the cathedral close by as I have lately formed the habit of slipping in before bedtime and there offering my closing prayers. Of course, I haven't shaken the habit of praying the minute my head hits the pillow, as well. But there God is apt to be short-changed as I quickly fall asleep!

The Catholic Priest

A lot of people, and this includes priests, feel that the great saints can point the way to an ideal discipline. They can help, but we should not make the mistake of trying to walk in anyone's footsteps but Christ's. For we are each unique and we each have to find our own path to God. I believe He has a distinct plan for each of us and we need to find it. So your daily discipline is going to be different than mine.

But a priest who has no discipline of his own is not prepared for the priestly life. It is a hard and difficult life and the number of Catholic priests, Protestant ministers, and Jewish rabbis who have nervous breakdowns is enough to warn us that no man can do it on his own. He needs God in his life constantly, and his life must be so disciplined that he runs no risk of going without God—or even of running too far ahead of God. Without question, *leading a disciplined life is the most important part of the priest's preparation.*

Next we need to examine one's academic preparation for the priestly life. There are a number of clergymen who have had little or no formal training. There are many reasons for this lack, including the idea that formal training is somehow just not necessary. Another is that the early disciples were simple men who had little or no education.

Let me address the second of these notions. It is not true that the early disciples and apostles were uneducated. Many of them were independent fishermen who owned their own crafts. As successful businessmen they stood socially—and educationally—a step above the common crowd. One has only to read the gospels and the epistles to realize the extent of these men's knowledge. They may not have gone to a formal school, other than the synagogue, but they *were* self-educated. The New Testament was written in *koiné* Greek by men whose mother tongue was Aramaic.

And of course Paul, as we well know, was a highly learned man. Modern readers fail to grasp the significance of Jesus going into the synagogue to read the Scriptures. This was in itself unusual. Most lay people of those times were illiterate. But Jesus was born into a carpenter's home where both the economic and educational level were just a step higher than a large portion of the population.

We hear talk of Jesus being poor, but the Scriptures do not bear this out. Only after He was called to preach did He put behind Him the security of the trade which His earthly father had taught him. But that is another topic. What is relevant is that He and His disciples were literate and had been exposed to more education than most of the people to whom they preached.

Now let me address the idea that education is simply not necessary. The Church of Jesus Christ is Universal. He preached the gospel to the poor, to the middle class—and to the rich. One of His converts, Joseph of Arimathea, provided Him with a tomb rather than have Him buried in the ground, as are all but the very rich. The Church is Universal and includes people of all nations, races, and social classes. A church which neglects the poor is not the church Jesus gave us. But a church which cannot reach the educated, wealthy classes because its clergy cannot communicate with them is also not the church which Jesus gave us. The uneducated preacher may *understand* the gospel as well as the seminary graduate, but he does not have the skill to *convey* this understanding to his educated parishioners The need to communicate the message of Christ is one of the principal reasons that both the Catholic Church and the main line Protestant Churches have long required such a rigorous education for those who want to serve as pastors and missionaries.

What kind of education is expected of them? Traditionally the Church has required proficiency in five areas. First, the priest must be a Bible student. Our faith and our theology are based primarily on the Bible. While personal experience, reason, Jesus, and the Church all contribute to our understanding, the Bible is where it begins. Further, the priest is expected by all to have a thorough knowledge and understanding of the Bible. Not to do so is to lose credibility in the eyes of his flock.

Secondly, he needs to have knowledge of the Christian faith to be able to present it in an organized manner. I found a good example of this importance in William Orchard's book, *The Way of Simplicity*. Orchard points out that the question, "What must I do to be saved?" has great theological implications. If we say, "Believe on the Lord Jesus and thou shalt be saved," we may have given the correct answer but the petitioner may not understand. Orchard says belief must be full and effective,[1] and that it involves four things:

> 1. We must believe what He says, all that He says, and so much that one does all that He says. Unless we obey and do all that He says, we cannot claim to believe in Him.

2. It means believing in Him, that is believing that he is genuine, that he means what he says and that He is what He says He is.

3. It also means believing on Him, that is giving up everything to Him, and leaning on His presence, and

4. It means believing up to Him, that is believing up to the full measure of faith, and believing that it is possible for Him to lift us up to His level.

In short it is not enough to utter a glib phrase like, "I believe in Jesus Christ and therefore I am saved." You have to know what it means to believe in all of its ramifications.

Truly faith without works is dead. To believe and not to do is a theological contradiction. And what do you mean when you say you are saved? Does it mean you will live with God forever? What is forever? If it is synonymous with eternity than it means that you will live with Him now as well as in Heaven. And if you are not living with Him now—if you are not living according to his laws—than how can you claim to live with Him in Eternity? Again it is a theological contradiction. Unless we are able to test our beliefs against sound theology we become people merely parroting phrases and slogans that have no meaning. By so doing we avoid answering the basic question, which is, "Are you truly living a life in Christ?"

The third field of study in the theological education of a priest is *liturgics*. I studied at the Lutheran Theological Seminary at Philadelphia, a school second to none. However, the man who headed the Liturgics Department was unable to bring life to his subject. In short he was boring. It seems incredible that anyone could make the study of the worship of God boring, but this man managed to do it. Although he was well versed in the mechanics of worship, he failed either to understand that worship had to come from the heart—or he was unable to communicate this central fact to his students.

After my graduation, I felt called to go into the Congregational ministry and my first parish was in the backwoods of Maine. The people in the parish had a church service almost devoid of any worship practices. The typical morning service consisted of a sermon, four hymns, some Scripture reading, and a few prayers. A very few prayers!

I looked at the congregation on Sunday morning and wondered why they were there. I also wondered if they knew why they were supposed to be there. True, they came to hear the word of God read and expounded in the sermon, but what provision was made for the confession of their sins, and the absolution which penitent hearts needed to hear? When did they have sufficient opportunity to thank God for His many blessings which He daily showered upon them? When were they given an opportunity to pray for the sick of the parish, for the mourners, the prisoners, and those who suffered from many misfortunes? But above all did they have an opportunity to give praise and glory to God? Yes, they had many hymns, but when we praise our fellow man we seldom sing our praises. No, it is more natural to voice our praises and to speak to God of His glory. Of course, we should do both.

Finally, what was most obviously missing was the one act of worship that Jesus had specifically commanded us to do. The Lord's Supper was observed in that church once a month and under some previous pastors less often than that. The Lord's Supper is the most intimate time we spend with Christ. Since the beginning of time, families and friends have drawn closely together as they partook of a common meal. Jesus and His disciples observed this common meal, or chabborah (i.e., fellowship supper), together daily throughout His ministry here on earth.

We can and should do no less. While in our work-a-day world most of us cannot attend daily Mass, the priest should and does, not for himself, or even for the small congregation that may share the Mass with him, but for the entire parish, those who belong to the parish, and for those who do not. The priest must have this sense of praying for the whole community, as should the congregation. A good seminary training must convey to every candidate for the priesthood that *worship of God is the most important function of man*: by voice, by song, and by deeds of mercy.

The fourth area of study for the priest is Church history. For many untrained pastors the study of Church history ends with the *Acts of the Apostles*. Although this is an important segment of church history, the Church did not end with the Acts. Many Protestants hold an interrupted view of Church history. They believe that after the *Book of*

The Catholic Priest

Acts was written, the Church which Jesus gave us disappeared. It became apostate and was not restored again until the Reformation.

The Mormons (or Latter Day Saints) hold a similar view, believing that the Church was not restored until the coming of Joseph Smith. This is a very peculiar and twisted view of Church history and of the Church. It says not only that they left the Church but that God also gave up on the Church. What happened to Christ's promise that He would be with us always? Neither of these things happened.

It is true that after Constantine, the influence of the state brought many unfortunate things to the church. Much of the church was corrupted by wealth and power, and most perverse of all, the Augustinian doctrine of the "just war" was introduced. But the overwhelming majority of believers were not corrupted by wealth and power, for they had neither. Even the Church recognized that its first line of believers, namely the clergy and the religious, could not participate in war, for war was contrary to their profession. Further, the church from Constantine to the Reformation produced some of its greatest saints.

The twelfth century was correctly labeled as the Age of Belief. People's lives revolved around their Christian faith, and the churches they built were everlasting monuments to how central faith was to the age. If even the most critical of Protestant scholars were to examine the faith of the centuries which they have chosen to ignore, they would have to admit that 95% of what was believed and practiced then is still believed and practiced by modern Protestants today.

Further, Christ promised that the Holy Spirit would lead and enlighten His Church. Surely, in all the centuries of His Guidance the Church must have learned much that needs to be studied, known, and practiced. During nearly two thousand years of history, as priests have listened to the confessions of the faithful, can anyone truly say they have learned nothing about the comforting and shepherding of troubled souls? A Church no more or less than any other institution can afford to ignore such a large part of its history. If modern Christians would only study what pastors for nearly two thousand years have learned about counseling, they would not be turning to the empty wells of modern-day psychologists and psychiatrists.

Finally, as students of the Bible we must be aware of how God's children have learned from the history of their dealings with God and God's dealings with man. Much of the Bible is history. And history did not stop with the publication of the Book of Acts. Christ intended that it should *begin* there, and so it did. A wise and educated minister will spend much time learning from history how God has dealt with His Church. He needs to study the lives of the saints, for they have learned much about God, man, and salvation, and it needs to be passed on.

Surely, one can learn more about the spiritual life reading about Meister Eckhardt than reading about the life of Hezekiah. If the modern Church has problems and if some of them are traceable to the pre-Reformation Church or even the post-Reformation Church, we need to know about them in order to set things right. God has much to reveal to us. Even as we individuals cannot accept that God is finished with us, neither is He finished with His Church. Before we can deal with the present and face the future, we need to study the past, for *God does not change and His ways of dealing with us and with His Church remain the same, now and forever.*

The last course of study is called Practical Theology, which simply means the application of theology to the day-to-day business of the pastor. All too often the emphasis is on the word practical rather than on the word theology. But a priest must always conduct his personal business and church affairs in accordance with the theology of the Church. He can not for example attempt to meet the church budget by raising funds through bingo, raffle tickets, and other means which are not consistent with the church's own teachings on Christian stewardship. You would not, for example, take money which you were holding for me and bet it on a horse. No Christian can bet because no Christian has any money of his own. It is all God's money!

The Sunday School has to be run not only as an educational institution, but as a Christian educational institution. When I was in Seminary, I worked as boy's worker at the Fifth Street Methodist Mission in the Northern Liberty section of Philadelphia. This was and is a very tough neighborhood, comparable to the Hell's Kitchen region of New York City. It had a large Sunday School of over 400 youngsters, and at one time there was a boys' class that was unmanageable.

One Sunday the class was given a new teacher, a silk mill weaver, and to everyone's surprise the class was not its usual, noisy, and rowdy self. After Sunday School, I rode home with him and a number of other teachers. One of them asked the silk weaver how he was able to manage the class so well. "Oh, I didn't have no trouble,"

The Catholic Priest

he said, "They started to get rowdy and I told them, 'Listen, kids, I am bigger and tougher than any of you and I'll knock the hell out of anyone that gives me any trouble!'" He was next asked what the topic of the lesson was, and he said it was the *Beatitudes*. I think we can agree this was not the "theologically correct" way to teach the *Beatitudes*!

Theology comes into almost every decision we make as priests. The many-divorced parishoner who is a large contributor to the church wants to be married again in the parish church by the priest. He would, if he could, buy a wedding. In most Catholic Churches he won't be able to do so (although, unfortunately, in the Roman Church in recent years it seems one can still buy annulments). There is in every act of the pastor a theological dimension, sometimes in places where it is unexpected, and sometimes the issues are bizarre.

For example, my professor in practical theology told of being asked to perform a baptism in a home. I am not sure why he would have agreed to a home baptism, but that was not the issue he found bizarre. When he arrived at the home everything was ready. The couple had even put the water in a large silver bowl that was to be used for the baptism. As he went to inspect the bowl he thought the water seemed to fizz and discovered that the couple had filled the bowl with champagne. It didn't take him long to explain to the couple that if the water of the River Jordan was good enough for Jesus, water would have to suffice for their son and heir, even though they could afford champagne!

Other common practices that violate sound theological principles are to allow politicians to speak from the pulpit and give a political speech rather than a sermon on the gospel. Nor does it make any difference if the politician in question is a clergyman, such as Jesse Jackson. Even if he promised during his presidential campaign to adhere strictly to the gospel, there are problems: whom would the congregation see and hear, Jesse Jackson the minister, or Jesse Jackson the candidate? The latter, of course.

One final note. One of the principal roles of the priest is his role as a pastoral counselor. He can fill this role in a variety of ways. He can take courses in all the latest methods of psychotherapy and with this knowledge counsel people, or he can learn all the latest methods in theological counseling and apply those things which he learned in the traditional courses in the cure of souls. If he does the latter he is being what he is called to be—a pastoral counselor. If he does the former he is a psychologist in priest's clothing.

A priest must always serve his people in a priestly role. He must never substitute any other kind of training or role for the one for which he was trained and to which he was called by our Lord, Jesus Christ. In short he must not sell his birthright for a mess of pottage. A *priest who knows Who called him and knows what he has been called to do will never seek to be anything but that person whom Christ has called.*

PART THREE
PRACTICE

X.

THE PRIEST AS TEACHER

Earlier we noted that the Pilgrims (i.e., the Separatists) divided the ministerial office into two parts. They elected for each congregation both a preacher and a teacher, and each role was as important as the other. In the earlier years of the Catholic Church an important member of each parish was the *catechist*, whose job it was to instruct those who were preparing for Baptism or Confirmation. Usually, the catechist was a layman, but today it is customary for the parish priest to instruct new converts and children preparing for first Holy Communion. There are some exceptions where a nun or lay person might prepare the children for their first Holy Communion, but by and large the pastor is the primary educator in the parish. A few larger parishes might have a director of religious education, but the primary responsibility always remains with the priest.

I always made it a point at the beginning of each year to tell the teachers in our church school that they were to answer every question that a child or an adult might put to them. If they were unable to answer it the pupil should be sent to the pastor so that he might answer the question. In short, we wanted no unanswered questions. But, if the pastor is expected to know Bible questions, theological questions, and all manner of questions concerning the church, it behooves him to continually study so that he may be able to do so with authority.

This all sounds good, but I do want to be more specific. In the chapter on education of the priest, I pointed out that it is very important that the priest know the Bible well. The Bible is the basis of much of our faith, and the public expects the pastor to be an authority in matters concerning the scriptures.

I have known clergymen who thought they knew a great deal about the Bible because they had memorized a great many texts and could without hesitation find a particular passage which they wanted to use to prove some theological position. We have had no great need to memorize Scripture since the invention of the printing press. Nor is it important to know where various portions of the scripture are to be located, since we have concordances to help us locate every single word of scripture. When I attended Sunday School, I had to learn every book of the Bible and be able to recite them in proper order. I am not sorry I learned them, but I am sure I would have done equally well now.

No, by "knowing" I mean *understanding*. It is rather odd that before Vatican II no Catholic woman would go into a church without having her head covered, but few Protestant Churches, especially the fundamentalists, followed the custom. Yet in Paul's first letter to the Corinthians, he admonishes women when praying to be certain their heads are covered. I am not certain why fundamentalist groups did not follow such a literal admonition. Catholics, of course, did it because it was traditional.

What does the priest answer when some woman reads the text in Corinthians and asks what she ought to do? A seminary-trained priest should know the answer, but if he doesn't he should be able and willing to consult a good commentary and supply the questioner with the answer. The reason for Paul's instructions have long since ceased to apply to any modern-day situation. Corinth was a large city, with a large athletic stadium and much commerce. It attracted visitors from all over the Roman World, and was noted for the many prostitutes who plied their trade in this cosmopolitan and prosperous city. They were out working in the early hours when Christian men and women were going to church services. The prostitutes went about with bare heads, and Paul was anxious that the Christian women not be mistaken for the "ladies of the night." Since we are not living in Corinth, and since even there the customs have changed in the intervening centuries, there is hardly any need to impose Paul's rule. In fact, in our society the ladies of the night are more apt to have the most beautiful and expensive hats. It is this kind of knowledge and understanding that the priest must be able to offer his people.

More importantly, the priest has to be a man of great common sense. Many people are frustrated in their approach to the Bible, and complain that there is so much they don't understand. But their salvation is not in jeopardy because of their lack of understanding. What we all need to be concerned about are those portions of the Bible we *do* understand, but do not follow. The priest's task is to make certain his

The Catholic Priest

parish offers a sufficient variety of Bible study courses to meet the needs of all but the most scholarly laymen and lay women of the parish. Further, Bible study for the average Catholic parish is an important evangelistic tool. Many non-Catholics long accustomed to hearing that Catholics were forbidden to read the Bible are attracted to Bible classes offered by Catholic parishes. When they come they find the Catholic approach refreshingly rational and scholarly.

The priest needs to be certain that he has a well-rounded and complete educational program in his parish. This is, of course, easier for a large church than for a smaller one. In the latter much of the education in Church history, liturgics, practical theology, and Bible must come from the weekly homily from the pulpit. I get tired of hearing excuses from pastors who when dealing with theological or Bible ignorance, say, "My people don't have any understanding of this." Why not? It is his responsibility to see that his people are informed about every area of faith and life, if not from the pulpit than from knowing about God.

Knowing about God is not the same as knowing God. All too often I meet people who know a great deal about the Bible, Church history, liturgics, theology, and they may even be familiar with the great devotional classics, and yet they have no faith. Worse yet, they do not know God.

During the 1930s a number of intellectuals were turning to the Catholic Church. They were attracted to the faith by such Catholic intellectuals as Fulton Sheen, and the Protestant world had difficulty understanding the phenomenon. It wasn't difficult, since people in all walks of life are seeking faith, and the intellectual looking for faith finds it easier to carry on a dialogue with another intellectual. Fortunately, the Catholic Church has always had a great variety of priests, including an elite corps of intellectuals who could challenge the secularism of today's intellecual educators and scientists. The Jesuits with their emphasis on education were ideally suited for evangelism among the intellectuals in our society.

However, the ordinary parish priest has only to have enough education so that he can have the respect of all the members of his parish. He also needs to carry his knowledge with a certain humility. I had a predecessor in one parish who drove away many parishioners because he talked down to them. I never had that problem; when I preached, I would pick out a twelve-year-old child and address my sermon to him or her. Because you keep your sermon simple and your vocabulary simple does not mean that your sermon lacks intellectual content. What must show is not your education, but your humility of presentation.

Jewish congregations expect their rabbi to be learned, and so they make certain he has time for study, and that he is able to keep up with the changes in society and in the religious community. It is important that the priest be a leader of his congregation. He must first keep up his studies, and, secondly, bring his congregation along with him. Every parish should have a good parish library, and members of the parish should be encouraged to subscribe to one or more good religious periodicals, including the leading journal of their own Church, plus at least one publication that will provide an ecumenical view of the entire Christian community.

While the priest may be the first teacher in the parish, he must never be the *only* teacher. He needs to bring in people from time to time from other parishes and from other denominations to talk to his own congregation. The Lenten season is an excellent time for this kind of activity. Wednesday night has worked for many parishes. The priest needs to choose a theme and find the best people he can to speak to his parish. He can trade off services with another speaker, or offer a small honorarium. But he should find them.

I also believe that the parish priest should always be the one to teach the confirmation class, whether it is comprised of children or adults. These not only are the most important classes in the parish, but they also afford the priest an opportunity to guide the parish in the direction it should be going. When his program comes up for review, he will get his best support from those whom he helped bring into the Church. Even more importantly, he needs to know the thinking, the hopes, and the expectations of every new member in his parish. If, as we have said, the priest is the servant of God and the servant of the parish, there is no better way for him to serve than to teach the Confirmation class. It is an opportunity and I have always found it a joy. If it is a children's class, it is especially helpful, since they will ask the questions the priest needs to address in his sermons. No other group of parishioners will be so honest and so open with him.

Finally, the priest will always remember that after prayer, study is his most important obligation to the parish. He prays that he

The Catholic Priest

might have devout parishioners, and he studies that he might have devout learned parishioners.

XI.
FATHER TO THE PARISH

Non-Catholics have difficulty with the title "Father" which is given to every Catholic priest. They cite Scripture to show that we are forbidden by Christ to call anyone "Father" except our Father who is in heaven. Yet, Jesus acknowledged Joseph as his father and all of us accord the title to our own sires. Apparently, Jesus used father in two different ways, and no one equates the two. To our Father in heaven there is no equal and when we refer to a priest as "Father," we use the title in the same way that we refer to a father who is the head of our household.

But since it causes problems for non-Catholics why do we insist on using it? The other choices have serious defects. Mister is much too cold, and using first names seems to ignore the dignity of the office to which the priest is called. A young priest, like Timothy, is often put down because of his youth. The older parishioner who comes seeking help needs the reminder that the title gives to the priest, and that he is, by his calling, by his training, and by his ordination, able to deal with the problems of his parishioners. He has by his ordination and the gifts that come with it become the father to his parish.

The care of each member of the priest's parish often begins at birth and ends with death. He is literally the father of his church. At the birth of each child the priest will visit the child and the mother to offer prayer, and to leave with the mother the office for the Churching of Women, which provides prayers of thanksgiving to be said in the hospital, and others to be said in the Church when mother and the child come home. The priest will call upon the mother and father after the mother comes home and arrange for the baptism of the child. Usually, families who are active in the parish will arrange for the child's baptism months before the child is born. Again let me point out the reasoning behind this. A child born into a Catholic family will have as a gift a

Catholic life from the day of his birth. The family will teach him about God, see that he learns to read, and present him with his own Bible. They will provide for a Christian education in the form of Church school, confirmation classes, and even Cana classes prior to his marriage. They will also provide godparents who will have a special concern for his religious life, and the parish priest will be a second father who has a special responsibility for his growth. The pastor may from time to time remind the parents that the child—and they—both need to attend church regularly. He is also there if the child becomes ill, or misbehaves and gets in trouble with the law. The priest is often found in court to give testimony regarding a member of his parish. He should be there, since he often knows what the court does not. He can give testimony regarding how solid the family is, the behavior of the child before he got into difficulty, and the support that can be expected from the parish and from himself, as the miscreant's priest.

Not all the testimony is so positive. I once was in court testifying on behalf of a parishioner who had been involved in theft. The judge had been given a psychiatric report which stated that the young man was a psychopathic personality. It become apparent to me that the judge had no idea of what a psychopathic personality was, and he proposed putting the man on probation. I asked if I could address the court and pointed out that we would be glad to have the man back in our community, but the court needed to address the psychiatric problem. When asked what I recommended, I asked that psychiatric care be made a condition of his parole, and I had the support of the local physician who was attending the trial with me. The judge said it wasn't necessary, as his parole officer could impose this condition.

Afterwards, when the man came back to the community, the parole officer came to see me and to tell me what he hoped to do for my parishoner. It was a sad event. The officer had been a former policeman who had been assigned to a race track. It was obvious he wasn't going to insist on psychiatric care; he knew less about it than the judge. It wasn't until the man stole an airplane that the court took the pyschiatric report seriously!

Priests often have to act as interpreters to the courts, local welfare officials, and lawyers. Even when the priest is required to reveal the worse side of his parishioner, he is acting as a loving father who wants only the best for his children.

The Catholic Priest

Sometimes, the role of father is restrictive, such as in the case of marriage. A young man or woman comes to the rectory with a girl or boy friend and they want to be married. Years of counseling experience tells the priest that they are not suited to one another. As a father he already knows that in this situation they will not listen to counsel. He does what he can to get them to look at their situation objectively—although he knows his effort is bound to fail. Having done this, like a biological father he smiles and goes ahead with the wedding.

In any case, if they choose to live in the same parish the priest, will be there to guide, instruct, and direct. He may be called in when the arguing gets serious, and when the problems get piled one upon another. That is, if he is lucky. No, I am not being facetious, for unless he is called in early, he may not hear of their difficulties until they consider divorce. Nothing is worse than to have a couple come into the study with divorce in mind, seeking last-minute, much belated counseling. On the bright side, because the parish priest is viewed as a "Father" to this fledgling family, he is often the first to hear of problems, before they become too large. And in his role as counselor to a marriage which didn't seem to have much of a chance, he may be able to work out the problems after all. No doubt before he performed the wedding, the knowledgeable priest will have prayed for a miracle!

What problems are of concern to the priest? All the problems that would concern a biological father. If the family is having a hard time financially, the priest may become a financial advisor. In one parish I spent untold hours as a job counselor, helping my parishioners find their first jobs, find new jobs, and counseling them on how to hold on to the jobs they had.

The role of the priest is unique. Many young men and women owe their education to the local parish priest. Young people of the new generation are often aware of their need to get more education than their parents. Sometimes a father will oppose this because he wants his son or daughter to stay at home and help him in the family business. Sometimes it is opposed because the father feels he made it without a great deal of education and his children ought to be able to do the same. The priest, as father to the parish, may intervene and try to persuade the parents to help their children reach their goals.

Often the mother will be the one to go to the priest, and ask that he speak with her husband. In many cases, she will demand that he exercise his role as father to the parish and talk with her husband. The priest has several advantages. First, he can be objective, whereas the biological father may have his own agenda.

Secondly, as an educated man himself he knows the value of an education, and is aware of the changing world in which we live. Parents tend to want things to remain the same, and find it difficult to cope with change. Because a priest is respected for his office, his advice is often heeded. Because he is called "Father," he can often accomplish what a cleric called "Bill" or even the cold "Mister" cannot.

He is a Father who serves his children from cradle to the grave. In the African Orthodox tradition many of their priests were also medical doctors, brought their parishioners into the world, and tended to their physical as well as their spiritual illnesses. Another analogy that is often overlooked is the priest's counterpart in Judaism. The Rabbi is the arbiter of first choice among Jewish families and Jewish communities. There is even a rabbinical court designed to settle many disputes within the faith rather than air dirty linen in a secular court. It is interesting that while the church for well over a thousand years used the religious courts for most disputes the increasing secularization of society left the religious courts only a few functions. Today many have become mere marriage courts, granting annulments according to canonical law. Even this court has lost much of the respect of the Roman Catholic community. We can learn from our Jewish brethren who did not allow the secular courts to be the only functioning courts in their religious community. But once again we are reminded that the priestly office has its roots in Judaism, and the functions of the priest and rabbi are not very different. The rabbi is a father to his congregation in fact, if not in name.

The hardest task of all is the one that seems to be the only function that secular society is willing to leave in the hands of the church, the task of burying the dead and comforting the bereaved. Even here secular society has made some disturbing in-roads. In many churches the funeral is not even held in the church building, at the funeral home. In cases of violent deaths the priest is no longer regarded as the counselor of first choice, but a new profession has arisen among the psychological community called "grief counselor." If the priest is no long the preeminent grief counselor, the church is in deep trouble and we need to revise our Seminary curricula.

Fortunately, most people in our society at the time of death in the family call a priest, minister, or rabbi. Frankly, no one else has anything to say regarding death. No one else can explain it, and no one else can offer any hope. This is not the time for evangelism, and anyone who uses it for that purpose risks losing the credibility that the church still has at funerals. The priest is the Father who will offer comfort to his children. He will remind them of the Scriptures they learned, and of the teachings of the Church that Jesus Christ was born to Mary and Joseph, and that he lived among men, and died and rose again to live eternally. And, finally, that Jesus offers us the same abundant life that he lived on earth and the same eternal life that he now lives.

A good Father gives good gifts to his children and the greatest gift of all is the gift of faith in Christ Jesus our Lord. And on this note we close. For all else that the priest does is insignificant to the Father's gift of faith to his children, the Children of God, his children in the Faith.

NOTE and BIBLIOGRAPHY

NOTE

1. Orchard, William. *The Way of Simplicity*, p. 17-19.

BIBLIOGRAPHY

Blackwood, A. W. *Pastoral Work*. Philadelphia: The Westminister Press, 1945.

Dicks, Russell. *Pastoral Work and Personal Counseling, Rev. ed.* New York: The Macmillan Company, 1949.

Galot, Jean. *The Theology of the Priesthood*. San Francisco: Ignatius Press, 1985, 274 p.

Hiltner, Seward. *The Counselor in Counseling*. Abingdon-Cokesbury Press, 1952.

Hiltner, Seward. *Pastoral Counseling*. Abingdon-Cokesbury Press, 1949.

Hoh, Paul J. *Parish Practice*. Philadelphia: Muhlenberg Press, 1956, 248 p.

Oates, Wayne E. *The Christian Pastor*. Philadelphia: The Westminster Press, 1951.

INDEX

Abraham, 15
Absolution, 23, 25, 64
Acts of the Apostles, 15, 64-65
African Orthodox Church, 80
Age of Belief, 65
All Saints Lutheran Church, Philadelphia, 46
Ananias, 9, 15
Andrew, Saint, 15
annulments, 67
anointing with oil, 51, 53, 55
Antioch, Church at, 8-9, 10, 16
Atonement, 24
Augustinian doctrine, 65
banns, wedding, 40
Baptism, 8, 15, 19, 49, 57, 67, 71, 77
Baptist Church, 36, 48, 49, 56
Barnabas, Saint, 8-9, 15-16
Baxter, Richard, 30
Baxter, William, 28
bereavement, 54
Bible, 62, 65, 71
Bible schools, 35, 73
Bishop, role of, 37
Blakemore, Dean, 27
Blood of Christ, 19
Body of Christ, 16, 19, 36, 40
Boston, mission, 10
Breviary, 60
Buchman, Frank, 8
Buddhist faith, 56
budget, Church, 66
Call to Holy Orders, 7-11, 57
        Jesus' call, 15
Calvary, 19
Cana classes, 40, 78
canonical hours, 59
Carfora, Bishop, 50
catechist, 71
Catholic Church, 15, 17, 25, 45-50, 67
Catholic Orders, 10
Catholic Priest, role of, 17, 31
chaburah, 18-19

China, 7
Christ Catholic Church, 10, 25-26
Christian Science Church, 52
Church at Antioch, 8-9
Church at Jerusalem, 9
Church of England, 45, 51
Churching of Women, 77
Commemoration of the Living, 55
compline, 59
Confession, 20, 23-26, 30, 64
confessional booth, 30
Confirmation, 8, 19, 57, 71, 74, 78
Contrition, 24
Congregation Christian, 9
Congregational Church, 9-10, 63-64
Constantine, 65
Conversion, 8, 15
Corinthians, 72
Cypress
Damascus Road, 7, 15
David, 15
Dicks, Russell L., 28
discipline, 58-61
Eckhardt, Meister, 66
education, 61-68, 71
epiclesis, 20
Episcopalian Church, 47, 49
Epistles, 36, 61
ethnic parishes, 46-50
Evangelical Churches, 9
Excommunication, 19
Fifth Street Methodist Mission, 66
Good Samaritan, 14, 42
Gospels, 35-36, 61
Gotthold, Jakob, 28
Graham, Billy, Rev., 49
grief counseling, 80
Grou, Fr., 60
healing, 51-56
Hebrew tradtion, 1
Hezekiah, 66
Hiltner, Seward, 29
Hindu faith, 56
history, of the Church, 64, 73
Holy Anointing, 214
Holy Communion, 21, 55, 71
Holy Living and Holy Dying, 27-28
Holy Orders, 7-11, 57
Holy Spirit, 8-9, 10, 15-16, 25, 36, 53-54, 59, 65
Holy Supper, 14, 16, 17-20
Hour of Decision, 49
The Imitation of Christ, 60
Instruction, 49

Italian Catholics, 46
Jackson, Jesse, 67
James, Saint, 15, 23
Jerusalem, Church at, 9, 10, 15, 17
Jesuits, 73
Jesus Christ
    life of, 58, 61, 77
    Sacraments of, 18-19
    priesthood of, 13-16, 57
    teachings of, 7-8, 10, 55
Jews, 13-14, 74
    rituals of, 20, 80
    society of, 17-19
John, Saint, 14, 15, 23, 45
Joseph Barsabas, 15
Joseph of Arimathea, 62
Joseph, Saint, 77
Judas, 15
Kempis, Thomas à, 59
Knights of Columbus, 49
Last Supper, 17-19
Latter Day Saints, 65
Letter to the Corinthians, 72
Letter to the Hebrews, 13
Litany for Peace, 60
Liturgical worship, 10, 18, 21, 31, 40
Liturgics, 63-64, 73
Lord's Supper, 10, 14, 16, 17-20, 29, 64
Lord's Table, 19, 60
Luke, Saint, 10, 14, 35
Luther, Martin, 28
Lutheran Church, 7-9, 30, 46, 49, 51, 55
Lutheran Theological Seminary, 63
Mark, Saint, 14, 45
Mass for the Sick, 55
Matins, 59
Matthew, Saint, 14, 15
Matthias, 15
Melchisedek, 15, 16
Messiah, 13
Methodist Church, 36, 48
missionary, role of, 45-50
Morman Church—SEE: Latter Day Saints, 65
New Testament, 7-8, 18, 25, 61
New Testament Church, 7, 45
Old Catholic Movement, 10, 19, 31
Old Roman Catholic Church, 50
Orchard, William 45, 60, 62
Orthodox Priest, role of, 17
Oxford Group, 8-9
Passover, 18
Pastoral Psychology, 28
pastoral psychology, 26-27

Paul, Saint, 7-9, 10, 61
        Calling of, 15
        Letter to the Corinthians, 72
        Letter to the Hebrews, 13
        as missionary, 45
Penance, 24-25
penitent, 26, 64
Pentecost, 15
Pentecostal, 36, 47
Pharisees, 14
Pilate, 14
Pilgrims—SEE: Separatists
Post-Reformation counseling, 28-30
Poustinia, 60
practical theology, 66-68
prayer, 58-60
preaching, 35-38
Presbyterian Church, 47
Priest
        as confessor, 23-26
        as counselor, 26-31, 79
        as father to the parish, 77-81
        as healer, 51-56
        as missionary, 45-50
        as preacher, 35-38
        as teacher, 71-75
        at weddings, 39-43, 79
        preparation for holy life, 57-68
Priesthood of Jesus, 13-16
prisoners, prayers for, 53
Protestant churches, 17, 30, 35, 47-49, 51, 64-65
Protestant clergyman, role of, 17
Protestant missionary, 45
Psalms, 15
Public Worship, Priest's role in, 17-21
Puritans—SEE: Separatists
Rabbi, role of, 17, 74, 80
Rahway, NJ, 10
Reformation, 45, 51, 65-66
Reformed Churches, 9
Restitution, 24
Revelations, 45
Roman Catholic Church, 30, 36, 46, 48-50
Roman Catholic Canon, 39
Roman Church, 24, 25, 45-46, 67
Romans, 13, 72
Sacrament of Confession, 25, 31
Sacrament of Marriage, 40-41
Sacrament of Penance, 20
Sacrament of the Mass, 14, 17-19, 31, 36, 53, 55, 60, 64
Sadducees, 16
St. Blaise's Day, 51
Samaritan woman, 56

sanctus bell, 20
Saul—SEE: Paul, Saint
Scriptures, 71-72, 81
Seminary, 9, 35, 46, 55, 63, 66, 80
Separatists, 30, 60, 71
Sheen, Fulton, Bishop, 49, 73
sick calls, 53
Simon, Saint, 15
Smith, Joseph, 65
Spiritual Maxims, 60
stewardship, 66
Stringham, Jim
suicides, 41-42, 54
Sunday School, 66, 72
Synagogue, 17-18, 20, 61
Taylor, Jeremy, 27-29
"Telling the Story of Pastoral Care to the Parish," 28
The Temple, 60
Temple at Jerusalem, 10, 14, 18, 20
theology, practical, 66-68, 73
Timothy, Saint, 77
Transubstantiation, 19
Tridentine Mass, 31
Unitarian, 36
Universal Church, 48-49, 62
Vatican II, 24, 31, 38, 47, 48, 60, 72
The Way of Simplicity, 62
Weddings, 39-43
"Whore of Babylon," 48
Zebedee, 15
Zhuraetzky, Peter, Archbishop, 10

ABOUT THE AUTHOR

Bishop Karl Prüter was born in 1920 in Poughkeepsie, New York. Following high school there he completed undergraduate work at Boston's Northeastern University, and then earned his master's degree in divinity at the Lutheran Theological Seminary in Philadelphia. After starting his ecclesiastical career as a congregational minister, he wrote two books, the second of which, *Neo-Congregationalism*, was later revised to include a chapter relating the personal sojourn that brought him to the Old Catholic Movement.

In 1967 Bishop Prüter was consecrated bishop of Christ Catholic Church, and the church, under his leadership, has significantly influenced the entire Old Catholic Movement. He has devoted much of his time to spiritual writing and to promoting the retreat movement. Throughout his work in the church, Bishop Prüter has conducted literally hundreds of retreats for both Protestant and Catholic groups.

Along with having written scores of religious pamphlets, Bishop Prüter has also written: *The Teachings of the Great Mystics, The Old Catholic Church, The Priest's Handbook, One Day with God, The People of God, The Mystic Path, Bishops Extraordinary* and has currently published his 12th edition of *The Directory of Autocephalous Bishops of the Apostolic Succession*.

He currently resides in Highlandville, Missouri where he serves the **"Cathedral of the Prince of Peace"**, which is listed in the *Guinness Book of World Records* as the world's smallest cathedral, measuring 14' x17' and seats 12 people.

St. Willibrord's Press

www.ingramcontent.com/pod-product-compliance
Lightning Source LLC
LaVergne TN
LVHW091315080426
835510LV00007B/506